LORRIES, TRUCKS AND VANS
1897–1927

LORRIES, TRUCKS AND VANS
1897–1927

PRINCE MARSHALL
DENIS BISHOP

BLANDFORD PRESS
POOLE   DORSET

First published in 1972
Reprinted 1979

Copyright © 1972 Blandford Press Ltd
Link House, West Street,
Poole, Dorset BH15 1LL

ISBN 0 7137 0598 1

*Colour Section printed by Colour Reproductions Ltd, Billericay
Reproduced, printed and bound in Great Britain by
Cox & Wyman Ltd, London, Fakenham and Reading*

CONTENTS

PREFACE

The problem arising from research is that the more one reads, the less one knows. Anyone having delved seriously into history – for whatever purpose – will have come out with conflicting opinions. It is never more true than in the limited sphere of this book. Easy it is for someone to say of a restored vehicle, 'All wrong – never had those lamps in 1925' or 'The first with that modification didn't appear until 1911', and similar arguments. But beware of know-it-alls! Study photographs, study documents, listen to all the voices possible – then you will become really confused! But after a while you will be more knowledgeable and able to render your interpretation of history. For interpretation plays as big a part in transport history as in any other.

Photographs, they say, do not lie – but they do strange things. A photograph might show a certain livery which only appeared for a week or so in the vehicle's life. Depending on whether the picture was taken on orthochromatic or panchromatic film is the degree to which the lining and shading shows up and the colour interpretation. Then again, the picture might have been taken with the specific aim of giving a false (ie, better) impression – not to deceive the historian but to present a certain picture to, say, a competitor or some other individual. Company records can be slanted – again perhaps to impress a competitor or shareholder, whilst it must be remembered that notes from which records were transcribed were often written by a clerk who was quite likely to make mistakes. History, therefore, can only be one man's point of view. As Henry Ford said, 'History is bunk'.

What you are about to read must be accepted in this context. I have spent many years studying and researching the history of trucks and buses – it has been my living for ten years and yet I sometimes feel I am no more expert than the next man. This book is only *my* interpretation of what I have heard and studied.

The first question that any book of this nature must answer is, where did it all begin? Who built the first commercial? And that is the most difficult question of all. Who discovered how to build the first motorcar was the subject of a long-drawn-out court case in

the United States and the question has still not been settled. Why? Because engineers, like historians, do not work in a vacuum. Ideas flow from one theory into another and there is usually someone to beat you to the post, sometimes by a day, sometimes by a decade, sometimes by a century. The motor vehicle was never the invention nor idea of just one man. Ever since he could express his thoughts, Man has wanted to move from one place to another in faster fashion and without being dependent upon a beast. But however much Man may have thought and secretly planned it was not until the British reform laws in the 1820s and 1830s and the birth of liberalism that he was freed from the restrictions placed on him by the State, and was able to devote his talents to improving his surroundings. Even then it was not easy. Opposition by the uneducated or the conservative-minded made life exceedingly difficult and it took another century for the majority to see that liberalism (capitalism) meant a better world for the many. To the engineer, opinions had to be backed up by *facts,* and however much the State might cry that machinery was an artifact of the devil, the fact was that machines turned the soil, extracted the potatoes and got them to the people quicker so there was less likelihood of their starving. Here we have the classic 'chicken or the egg' situation. Did man's determination not to starve produce the motive power or did motive power enable a world to be built where man need not starve? Whichever the case, the commercial vehicle was the number one tool in a new society structure, although it took a number of decades after the birth of capitalism before motorised commercial vehicles freed themselves from the idea of the steel wheel to steel rail! A society with a history of years of collective thinking still operated in terms of bringing together lots of trucks and taking them from A to B, rather than letting Z go to M, C go to F, R go to A, and so on. It took precisely 100 years to realise fully that the most effective method was to have lots of motorised trucks going out at a moment's notice, rather than when they had all been gathered together.

This book is primarily about trucks and vans of the period up to 1927. Reference is often made to buses because up to the middle twenties both types of vehicle were made on the same chassis, and very often trucks grew as a sideline for manufacturers whose original purpose when starting their business had been buses. Fire engines are to be dealt with in a book of their own in this series later on.

Some readers may be disappointed at not seeing their favourite

vehicle illustrated in this book, but in a volume of this size it is not possible to include one hundredth of the makes of vehicles built during the period. Denis Bishop and I have shown just a sampling of the types seen. Many even of our own favourites have had to be omitted.

In conclusion I would like to offer my sincere thanks to Arthur Ingram for his great assistance and to professor Brian Firth, University of Nevada, for having put me right on so many points. With both these gentlemen I have enjoyed sharing the joy of learning about trucking over the past twenty years. And, of course, my thanks to my wife, who patiently typed the whole manuscript and has had to listen to truck jargon morning, noon and night!

Prince Marshall

A TOAST TO THE TRUCK

Once upon a time the paper money of the English-speaking countries was as good as gold; a liberal was adamantine in insisting upon free trade; a conservative believed that any asset, such as man's life or fortune, was best conserved by its owner. In those days, which all must admit were old – fifty years ago? – and some of us hold were good, in those days it was the mark of an educated man to respect the 'law of supply and demand', to accept that any attempt to give people what they did not want, or to deny them that which they did want, was simply an attempt to substitute might for right, the power of the sword for that of the pen, and therefore doomed to failure.

The history of the truck is one of a triumph over prejudice and oppression. Truck speeds have been limited to that of a man on foot, to 12 mph, to 20 mph, to 30 mph, to 40 mph. The gross weights and axle loads of trucks have been limited. And then the trucks have been vilified because they have only small engines and cannot keep up with other vehicles on hills! Today not only the weight that the tyres may place upon the road, but the design of vehicles is decided by outside authorities who do not ride on the vehicle, nor depend upon it for their living. It is hard to see any opportunity for a particularly gifted driver or manager to improve his performance and give a better service to the customers. Indeed, if someone tomorrow divined a way to double the power output of the engine or the load-carrying ability of the tyres, the customers would not beat a pathway to his door, because the 'right' to serve a certain route is awarded not by the customers but by the Government.

But despite the fact that the odds have been stacked against it, that it has had no chance to develop its full potential, the truck has seized the lion's share of inland traffic and shows no sign of letting go. The 'Hovercraft' has not revived the canal network. And railways continue to go bankrupt.

Because the truck has a driver, it needs only the simplest of permanent ways, a mere strip of hard going with some friction, to connect a farm or a quarry or a mine or a dock or a forest into a

transportation system which embraces all our markets and stretches throughout the land, and even – with drive-on, drive-off ferries – overseas.

The truck can tolerate failures. On an aircraft or a train there are many things which simply must not fail. So these things must be made very expensively, or else replaced long before they are worn out. But the truck can be fitted with devices of very high performance because the driver will be able to adapt to the changed conditions when they fail; the truck can have exhaust brakes and transmission retarders, and can rely upon that exceedingly subtle stroke of genius, the pneumatic tyre. Only one railway, the Paris Metro, exploits the high traction and gentle guidance afforded by the pneumatic tyre, and the tyres it uses were developed to the necessary high reliability by service on road vehicles.

It does not need a traffic control system to follow the movements of the vehicles – the driver finds his own way. This function is so simple that it is often overlooked – until one discovers that on a railway a load is sent off and then all trace of it can be lost until it arrives! Henry Ford I, who seldom wasted a cent, found it worth while to have his own men all over the railroads, watching for cars consigned to Ford Motor Company and making sure that they went there . . . pronto!

The capital charges in trucking are low – the costs are largely wages and fuel and tyres and repairs, the costs which go on even when the truck is not running are small. And this is important indeed. It means that the truck is not confined to traffics which can be estimated with confidence and expected to last for years, it can seize opportunities and do jobs which may last only weeks or months.

And a system with relatively low capital charges is at an advantage even if the traffic can be relied upon to continue into the far future, perhaps bringing coal to a base-load power station. (A quite typical power station may have eight *miles* of railway sidings, to safeguard itself against a railway strike; at normal power, it may need to be served by one 5-ton truck every minute.) Systems which are highly 'efficient' but very costly to build, such as canals or electric railways, are virtually never able to earn enough money fast enough to scrap the original installation and put in a better one. The truck, with its low capital costs, stands at the other extreme; trucks are replaced in a few short years, and hence new ideas spread rapidly.

A visit to any of the functions of the Historic Commercial Vehicle Club will show how true this is; the trucks of only twenty years ago are now curiosities, being reminisced over by fathers to sons. And there is one respect in which improvement is most conspicuous. In those good old days, the engineer had all he could do to keep the truck running, and stopping, in service: the engineer relied upon the driver not only to demonstrate good judgment and adapt to changing circumstances, but also to endure. The driver was expected to be strong enough to work the brakes and the steering by main force (though sometimes with the assistance of very ingenious mechanisms – who that has ever heard it can forget that most romantic of sounds, the musical, metallic clang as a ratchet handbrake is knocked off and a heavy truck rolls out into the lonely, distant dark?) He was expected to be determined enough to peer through badly swept screens of curved glass. He was expected to resist heat in summer and cold in winter, to be unaffected by noise and by fumes. But now we see cabs which are fully enclosed and ventilated or heated, effective and not haphazard means to keep the engine from making its presence felt, seats which are both comfortable and adjustable, controls which are convenient for the driver rather than for the draughtsman. The designers, perhaps only under the pressure of artificially intense competition, have recognised that the driver is the most important feature of the vehicle.

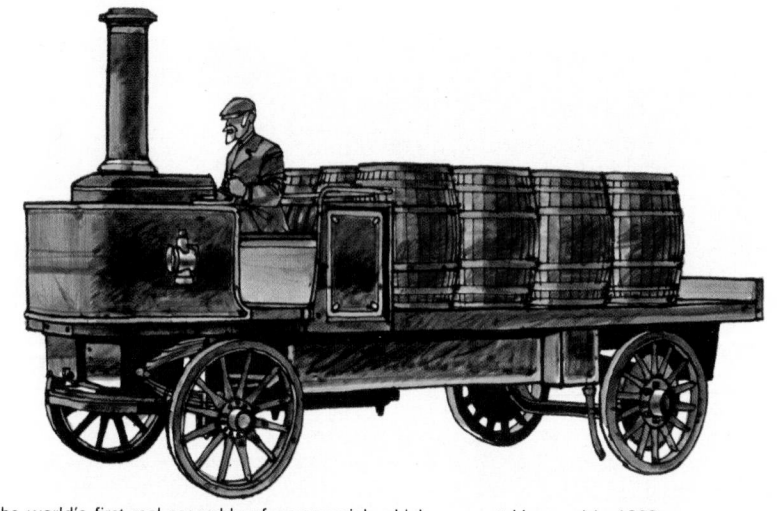

1

The world's first real assembly of commercial vehicles was at Liverpool in 1898,
organised by The Self-Propelled Traffic Association. Of the handful that turned
up the vehicle to put on the best show was this oil-fired 2-ton wagon built by
THE LIQUID FUEL ENGINEERING CO (LIFU).

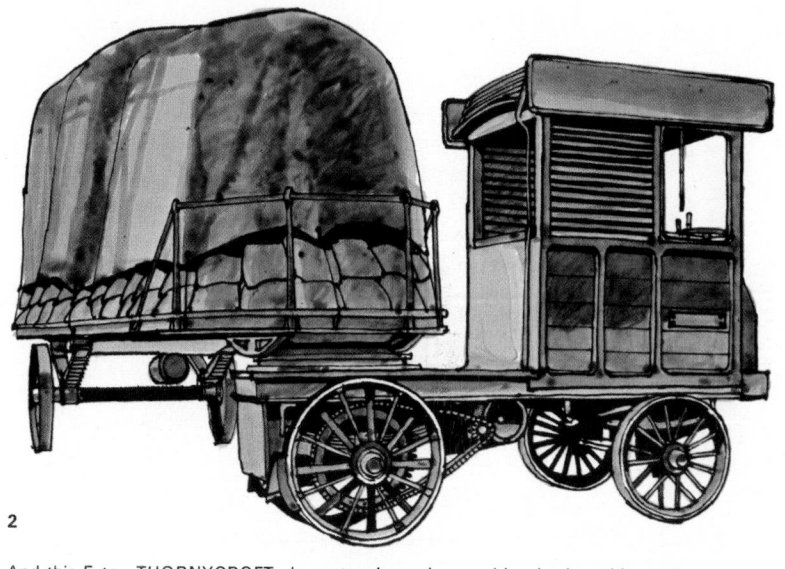

2

And this 5-ton THORNYCROFT also entered was beset with wheel troubles and
a burst tube. That aside, it was the first articulated goods vehicle and probably the
first designed to carry a 5-ton load.

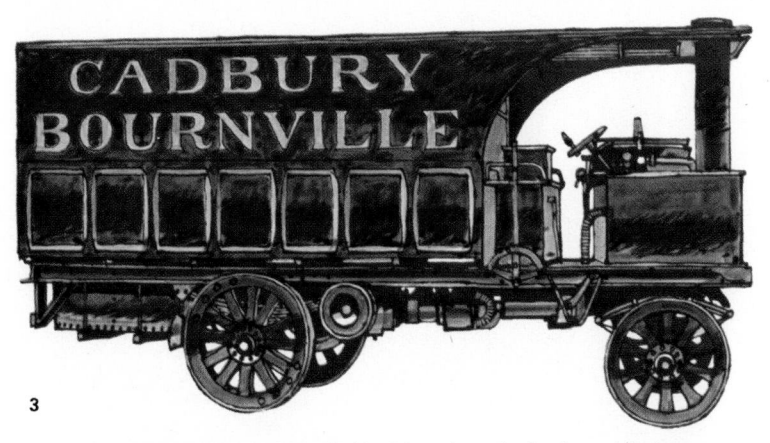

3

By 1902 THORNYCROFT could justifiably claim to be at the forefront of the heavy lorry business. They had gained immense experience, having entered all the trials (civil and military) for self-propelled vehicles.

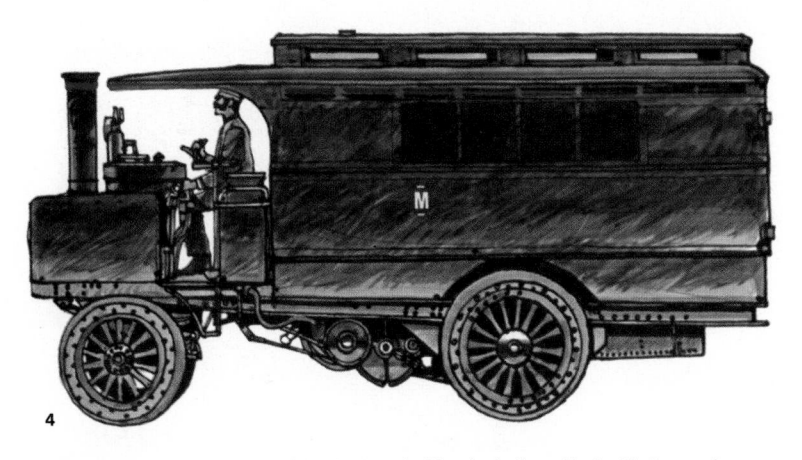

4

They offered every type of body imaginable, including Black Marias and ambulances.

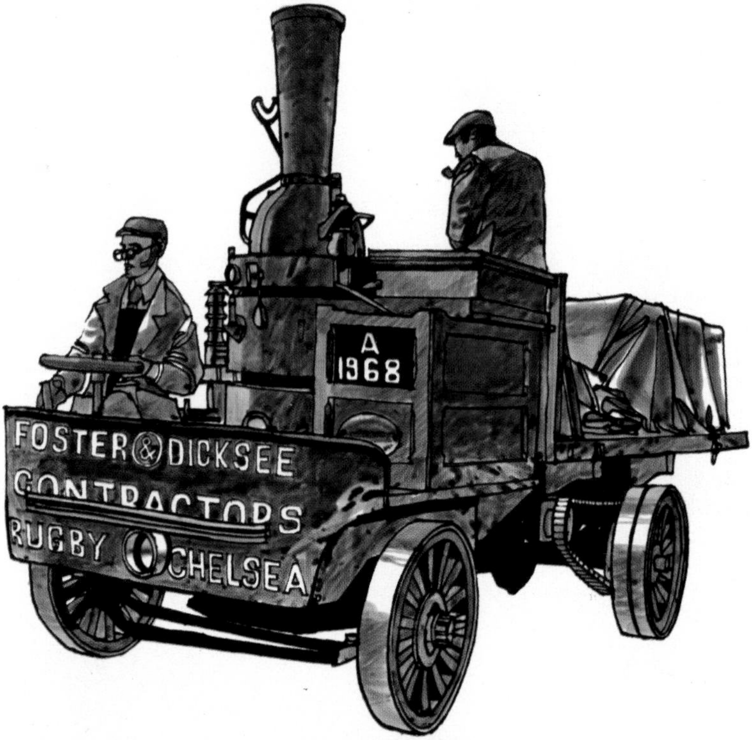

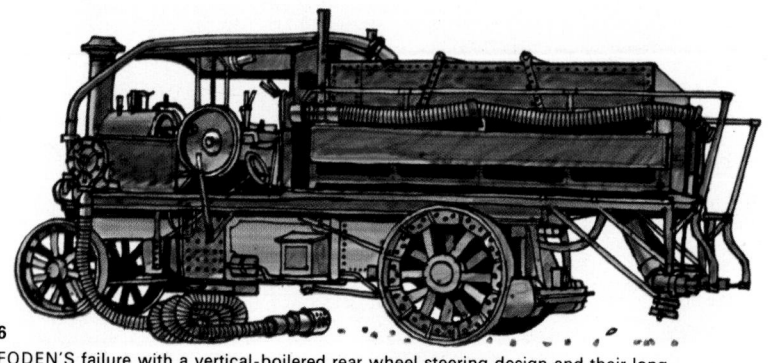

5

T. COULTHARD & CO of Preston were responsible for 50% of the share capital in J. Sumner Ltd (later Leylands) in 1895. After a disagreement Coulthard pulled out and manufactured their own rival wagons, but Leyland triumphed in 1907 when they absorbed Coulthard. This Coulthard wagon is said to have delivered every single piece of stone for the erection of the new War Office building at Whitehall in 1904.

6

FODEN'S failure with a vertical-boilered rear wheel steering design and their long experience with traction engines re-affirmed their belief in the loco-type boiler when they got down to serious wagon production after 1900.

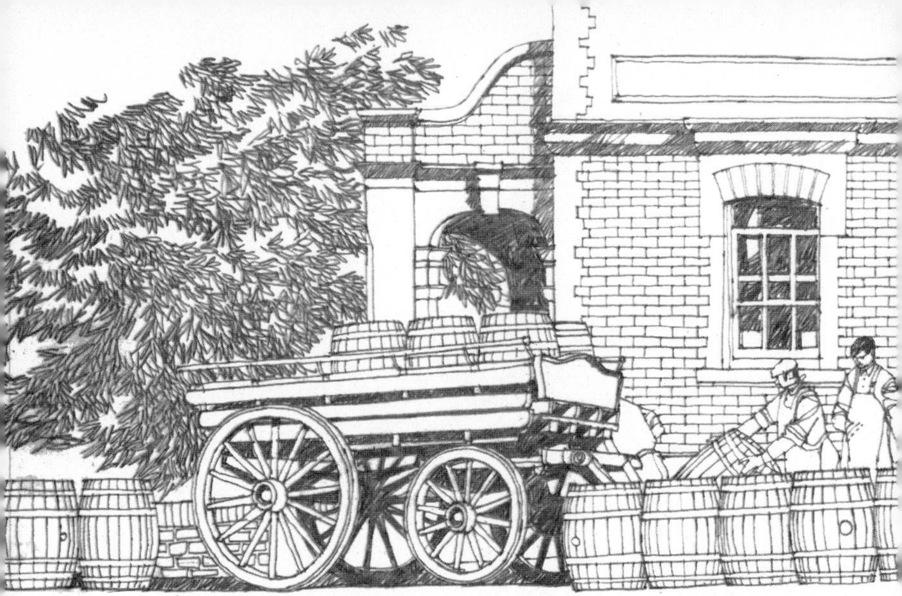

7 Fodens found a ready market with the breweries who were among the first firms to display their faith in the steam wagon. Note another influence of the railway locomotive—the rear suspension, only seen on the earliest of Fodens.

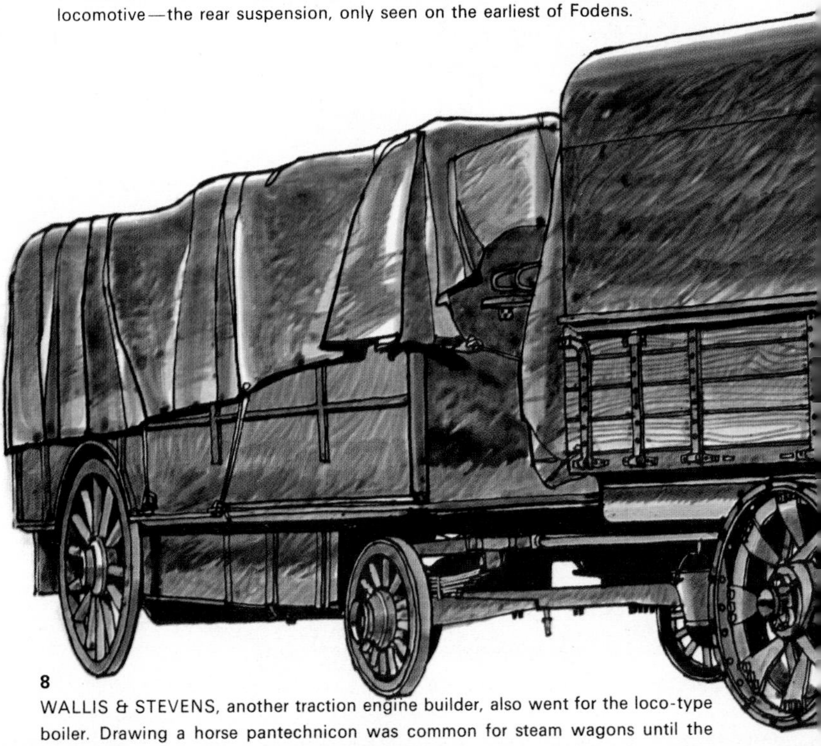

8
WALLIS & STEVENS, another traction engine builder, also went for the loco-type boiler. Drawing a horse pantechnicon was common for steam wagons until the early twenties.

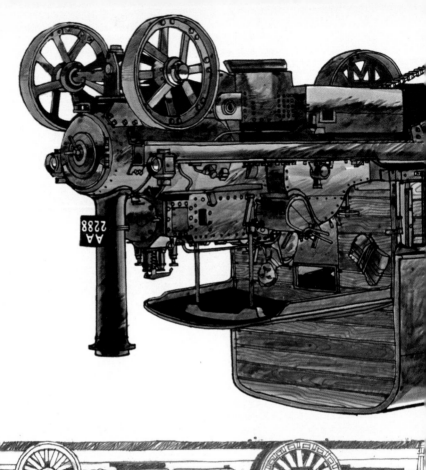

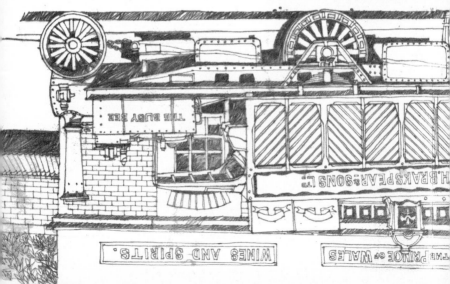

The locomotive boiler was not so popular in hilly districts particularly when parked on a steep gradient and the fire tubes were left to dry. One of the Mann family in Leeds patented the transverse boiler and eventually set up production of the YORKSHIRE wagon. There were only two firms to concentrate on the transverse boiler principle and Yorkshire became the most popular.

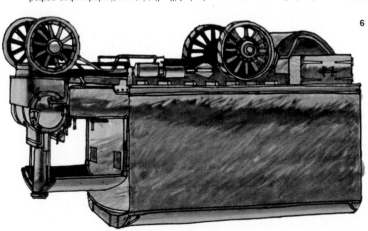

9

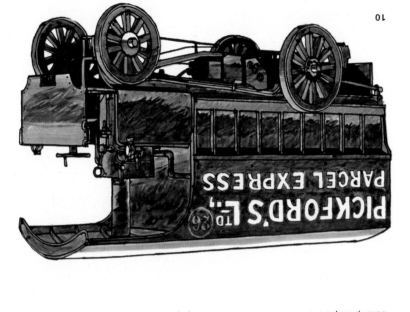

10

A short-lived firm called ENGLISH chose the vertical position. It was the vertical boiler position that most firms eventually tried their hand at in the twenties, although mounted lower in the chassis frame.

In the United States the steam wagon never gained any popularity—emphasis was on lighter-constructed vehicles, usually electric. An air-cooled 2-cylinder opposed engine propelled this HOLSMAN. The high wheels, although derived from the horse buggy, were supposed to stop the undercarriage from getting damaged if the vehicle got bogged down on country roads.

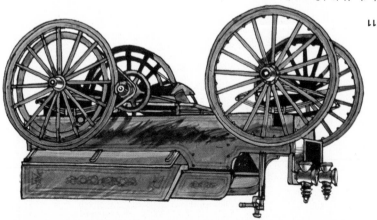

11

Fastest selling and perhaps most reliable of all early American automobiles was R. E. Olds' OLDSMOBILE. The truck division was not set up until 1904 but many curved-dash car chassis were turned out with 'pie-van' bodies like this one.

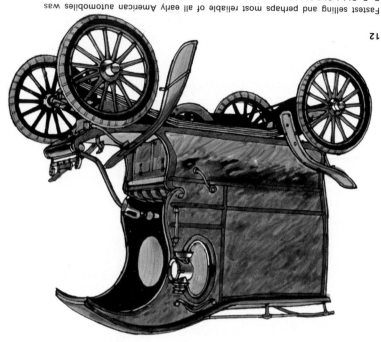

12

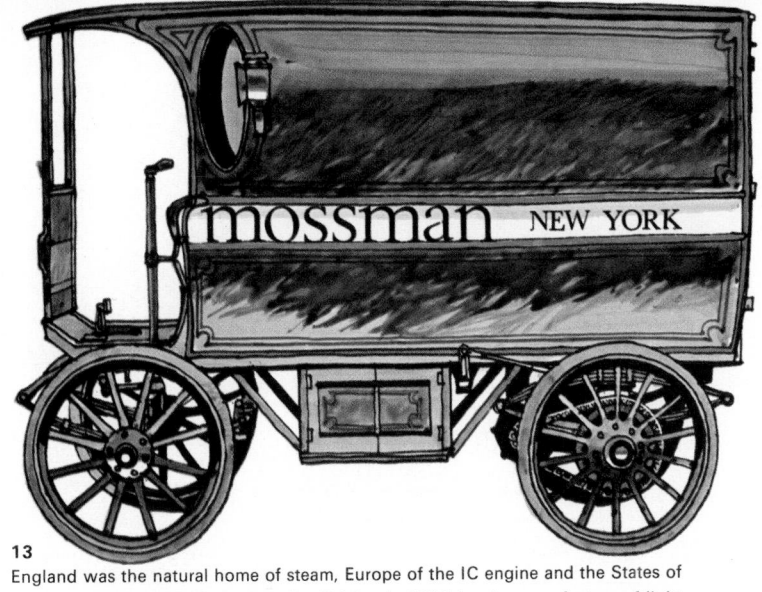

13

England was the natural home of steam, Europe of the IC engine and the States of the electric. STUDEBAKER started a division in 1905 for the manufacture of light electric vans and trucks.

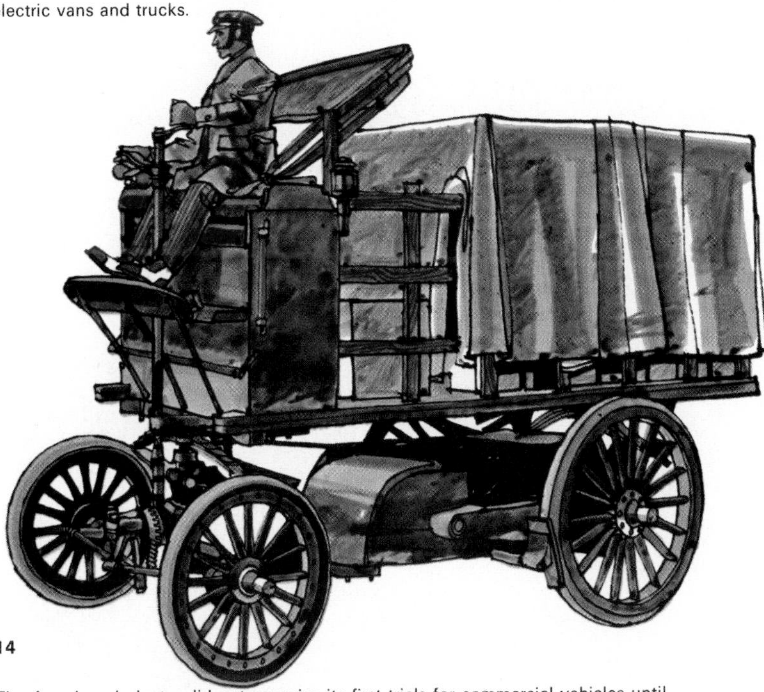

14

The American industry did not organise its first trials for commercial vehicles until 1903 and these were held in New York. Among the 14 entries, one of which was a British Coulthard steam wagon, was this primitive-looking UNION, made in Union City, Indiana.

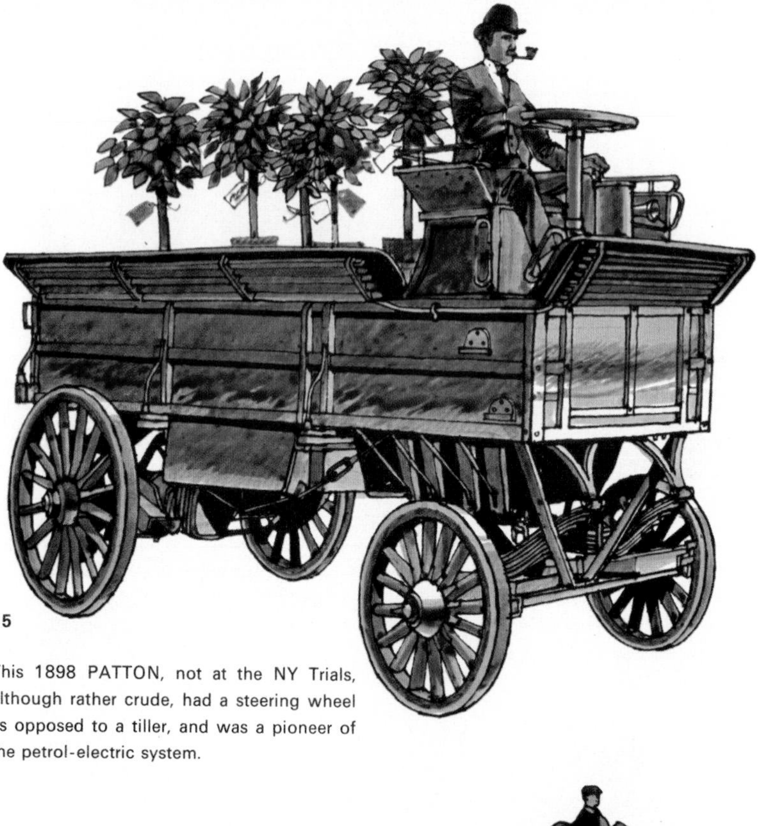

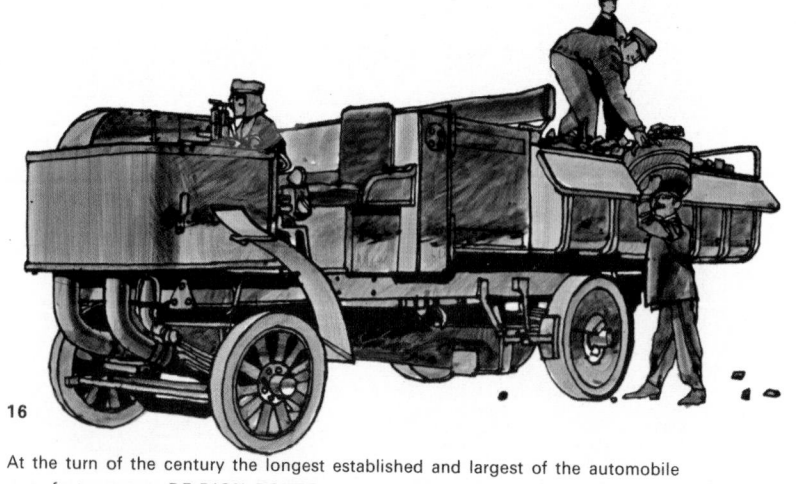

15

This 1898 PATTON, not at the NY Trials, although rather crude, had a steering wheel as opposed to a tiller, and was a pioneer of the petrol-electric system.

16

At the turn of the century the longest established and largest of the automobile manufacturers was DE DION-BOUTON. Their origins dated from the early 1880s. From around 1899 they concentrated on their single-cylinder petrol engine for the propulsion of the cars and light commercials, and steam power for the heavy range, such as this Paris dustcart.

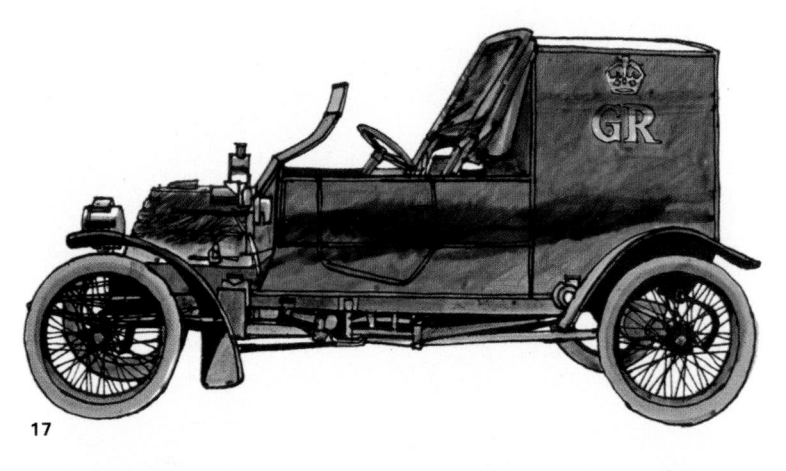

17

De Dion's single-cylinder cars outsold any other manufacturer at the turn of the century. The firm also had a wide market selling loose engines. This gave many individuals and firms the chance to build vehicles without the expense of tooling for engine production. This amateur-built post van was built by Mr T. Spencer of Gainsborough in 1900.

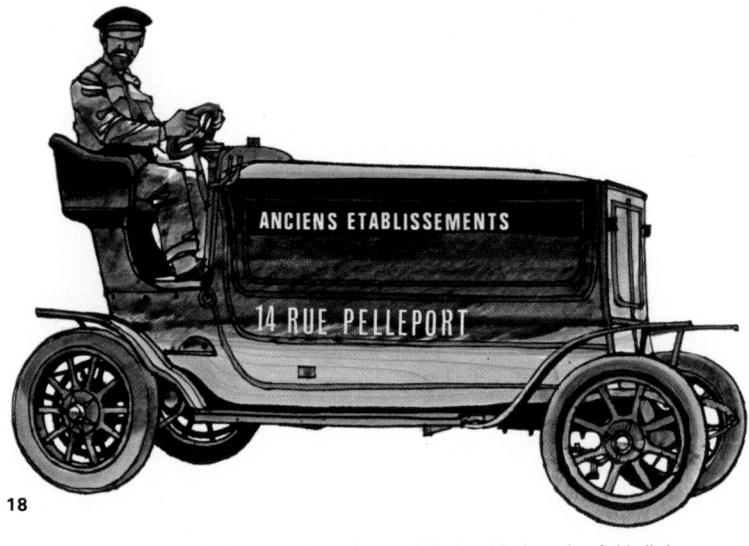

18

ROVAL had a brief spell of success in and around Paris with the sale of this little grocer's delivery van—again fitted with the 6hp De Dion engine.

The French were first with their *Poids Lourds* contest in 1897, organised by the ACF, although they abandoned them between 1901 and 1904. The 1906 *Poids Lourds* trial, held in June, was over 555 miles from Paris via Compiegne, Amiens, Dieppe, Le Havre, Rouen, Marius, and back to Paris. Fifty-seven vehicles completed the run, among them the Paris made GUILLIERME.

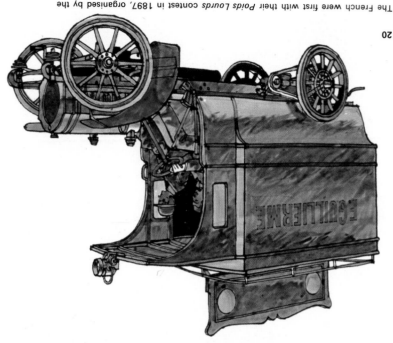

20

One of the few European steamers to hit the limelight was the DARRACQ-SERPOLIET with its two simple double-acting horizontal cylinders. Those that came to London on bus work failed to sustain steam pressure for a good day's work.

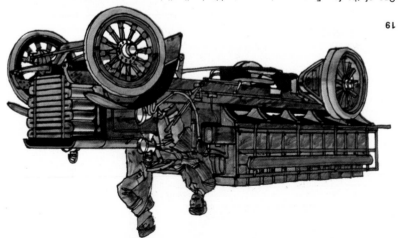

19

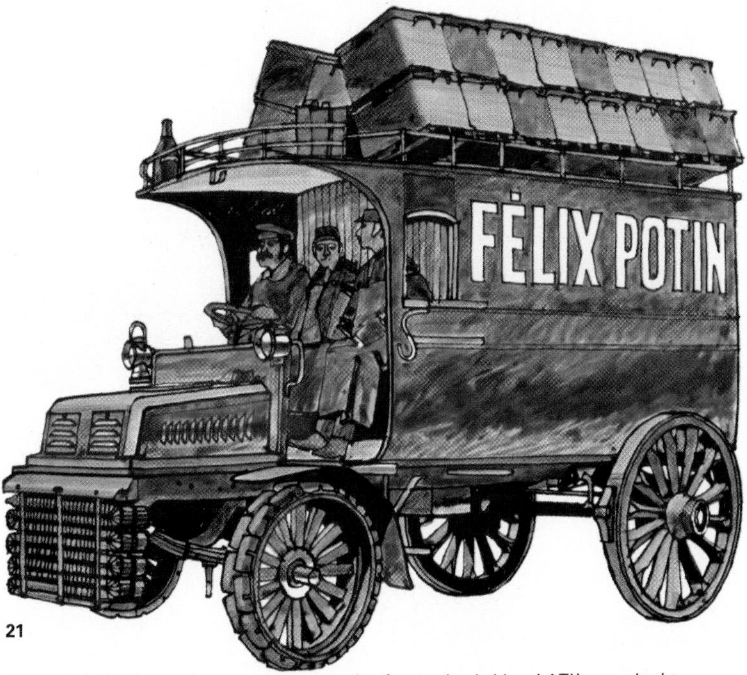

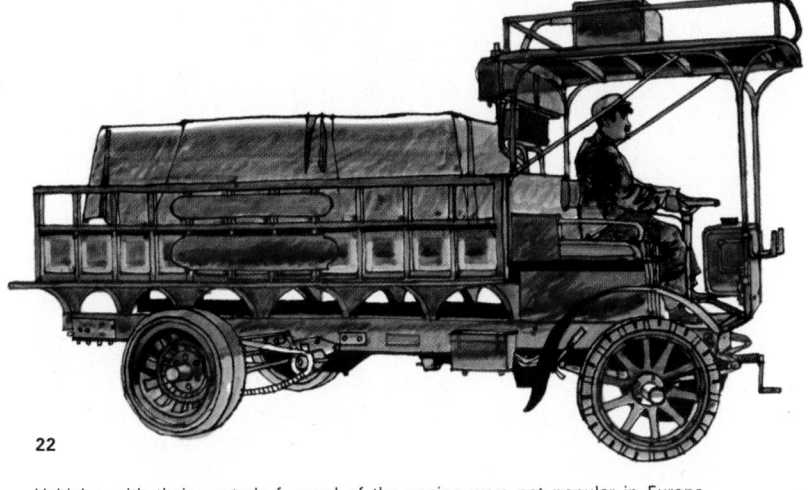

21

A good deal of attention was given to the front-wheel-drive LATIL, no doubt warranted in view of their subsequent long success with the renowned four- and front-wheel-drive vehicles.

22

Vehicles with their controls forward of the engine were not popular in Europe. This French-constructed ARIES of 1906 also took part in the Paris Commercial Vehicles Trials.

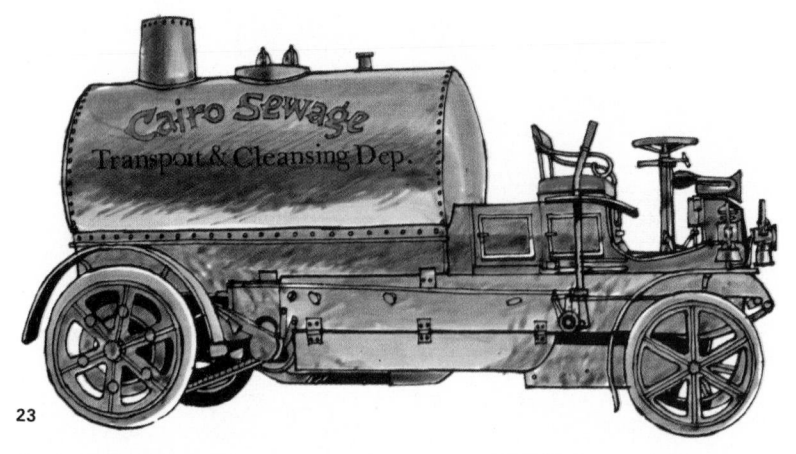

23

The Swiss-built ORION was truly advanced in design. It had a 2-cylinder horizontally opposed underfloor engine. Reasonable numbers were sold and in Britain they were marketed by Moss & Woodd at Cricklewood, London.

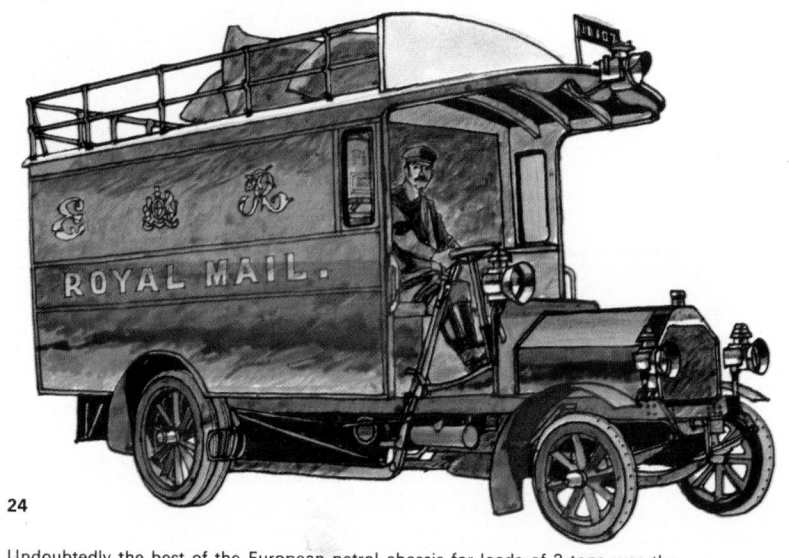

24

Undoubtedly the best of the European petrol chassis for loads of 3 tons was the MERCEDES-DAIMLER built in Marienfelde, Berlin. Those built under licence in Britain by the tramcar builder, G. F. Milnes, were MILNES-DAIMLERS.

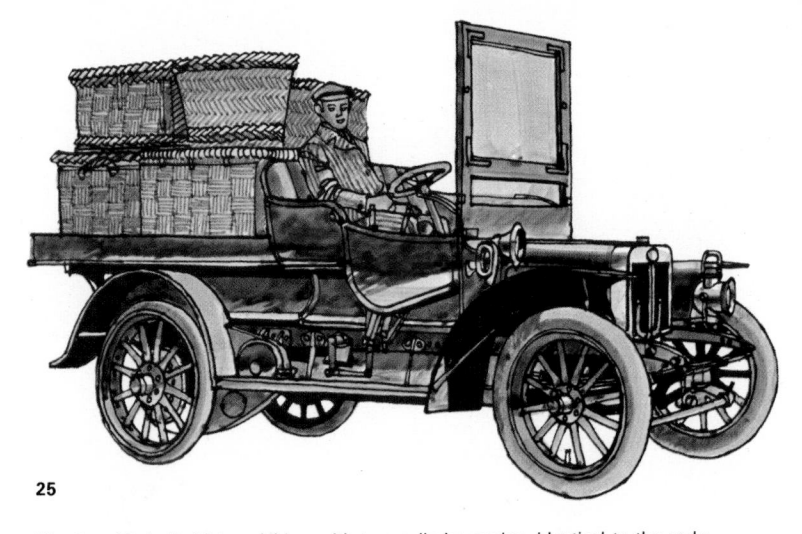

25

The Scottish-built 16 h.p. Albion with two cylinder engine, identical to the early chassis sold by Lacre, was considered the most reliable small vehicle on the British market before the First World War.

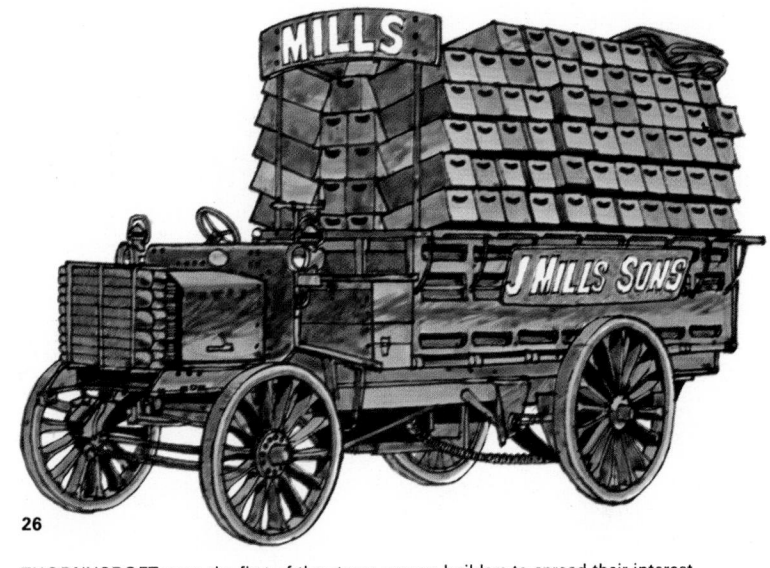

26

THORNYCROFT were the first of the steam wagon builders to spread their interest into the petrol field. Petrol lorries were made to take loads up to 2 tons from 1902.

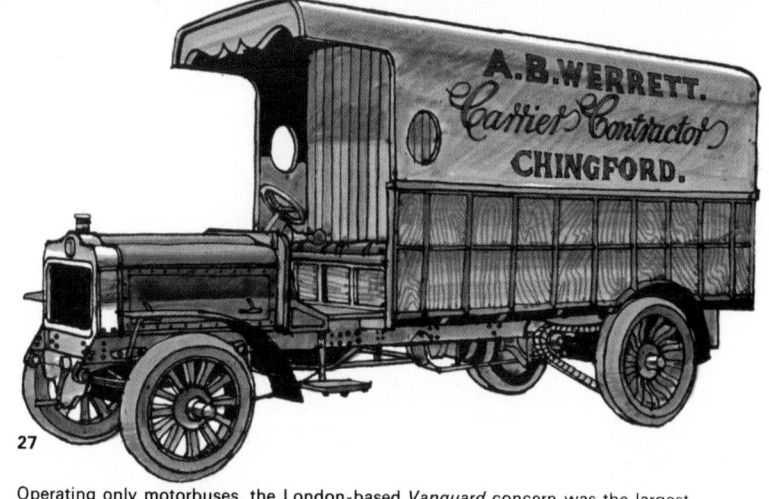

27

Operating only motorbuses, the London-based *Vanguard* concern was the largest such company in Britain through 1906 and they intended to use their operating expertise to manufacture buses. For that purpose they set up the MOTOR OMNIBUS CONSTRUCTION CO at Walthamstow. Some MOC chassis were sold as vans.

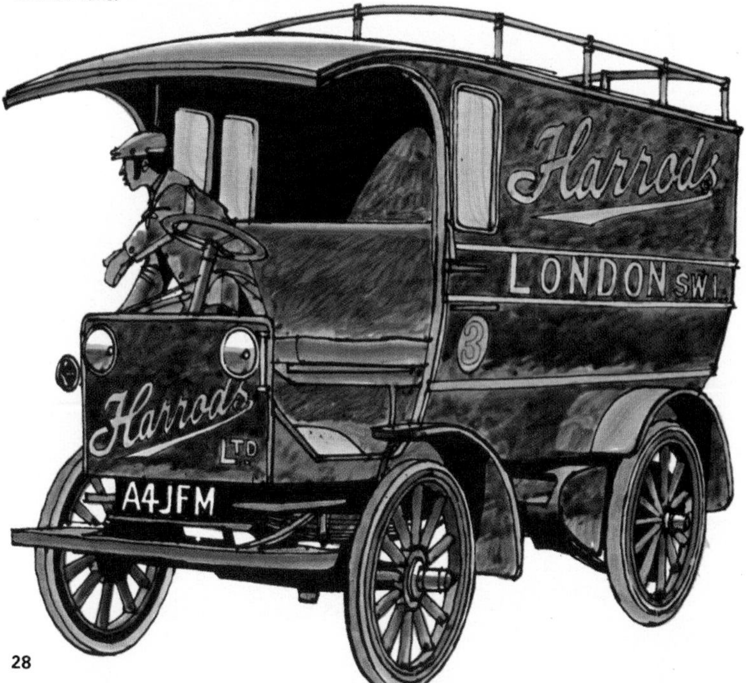

28

One of the first users of electrics in Britain was the famous Harrods store. At first they were American imports and then of British manufacture, but under licence. In later years Harrods manufactured their own vehicles from component parts.

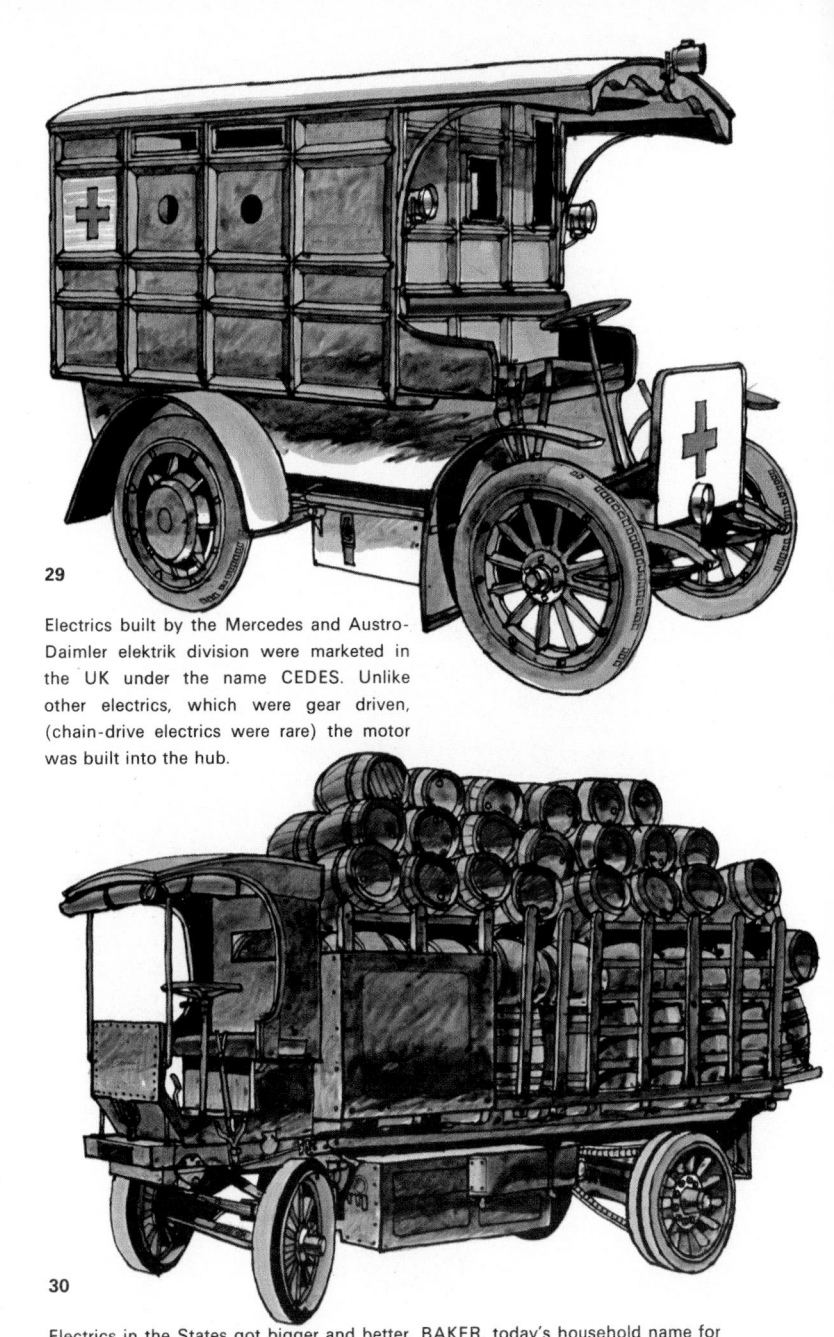

29

Electrics built by the Mercedes and Austro-
Daimler elektrik division were marketed in
the UK under the name CEDES. Unlike
other electrics, which were gear driven,
(chain-drive electrics were rare) the motor
was built into the hub.

30

Electrics in the States got bigger and better. BAKER, today's household name for
industrial fork-lift trucks, began life in 1908 marketing electric trucks of exceptional
quality and value.

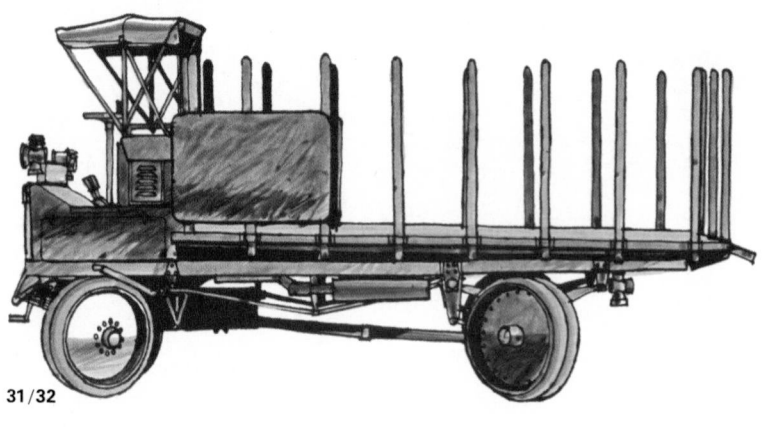

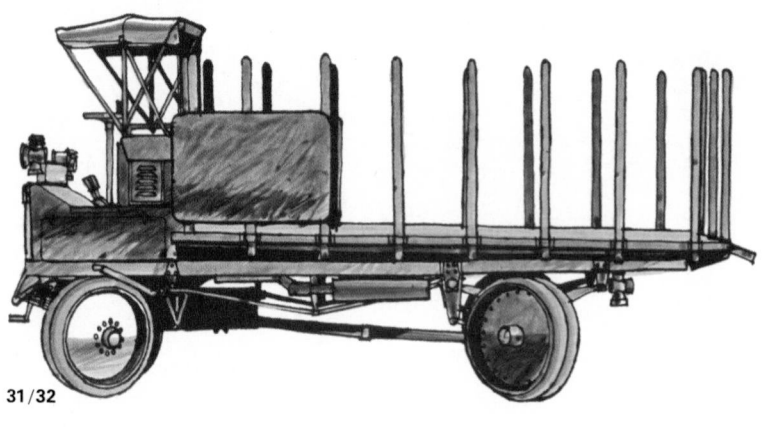

An idea that must soon be rediscovered and announced as the wonder of the age: the COUPLEGEAR had a four-cylinder petrol engine, providing the power for four independent electric motors, one mounted on each wheel; additionally all four wheels steered. The couplegear was one of America's foremost electrics *c*. 1910–1918.

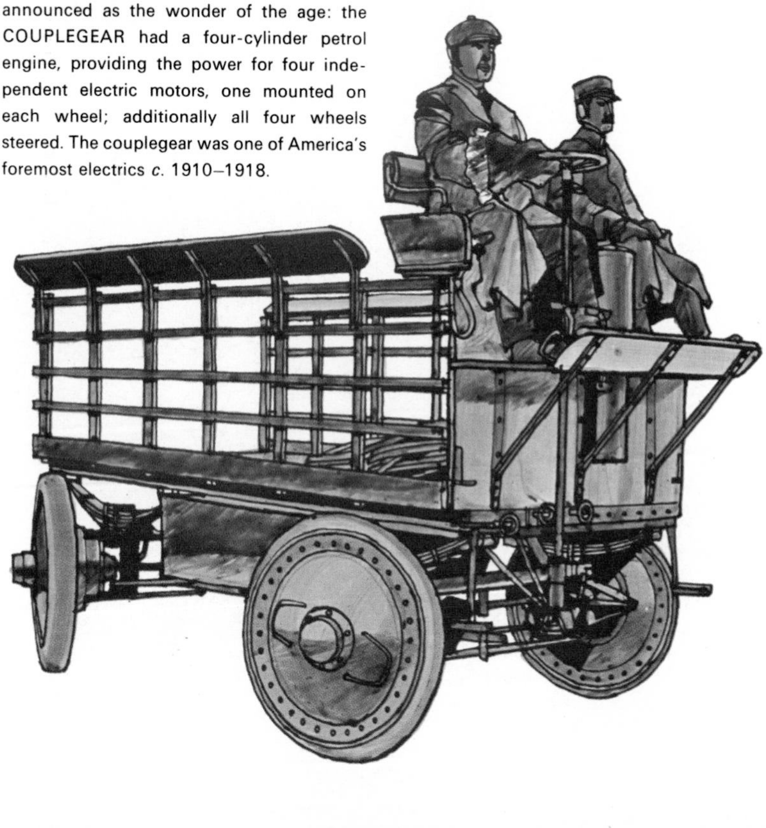

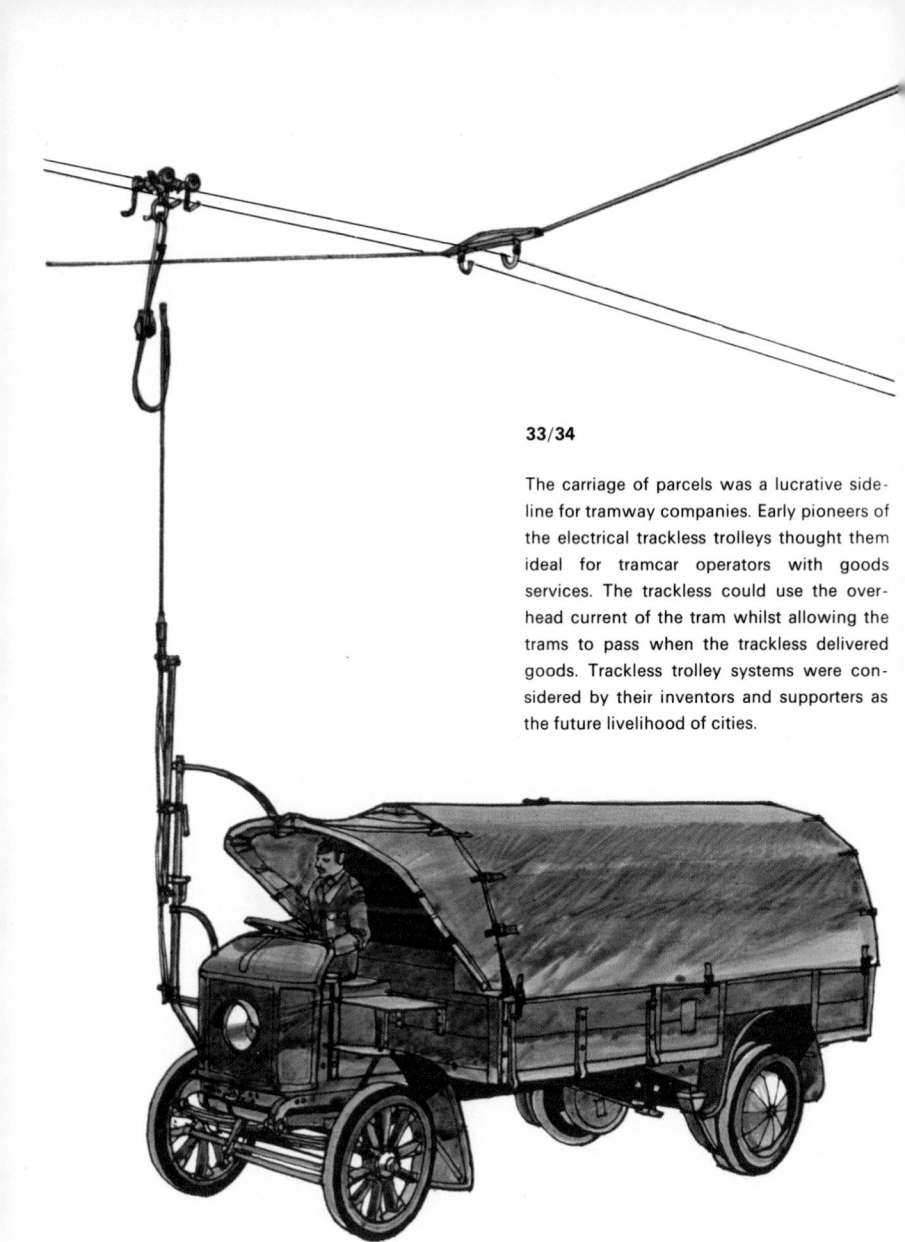

33/34

The carriage of parcels was a lucrative side-line for tramway companies. Early pioneers of the electrical trackless trolleys thought them ideal for tramcar operators with goods services. The trackless could use the overhead current of the tram whilst allowing the trams to pass when the trackless delivered goods. Trackless trolley systems were considered by their inventors and supporters as the future livelihood of cities.

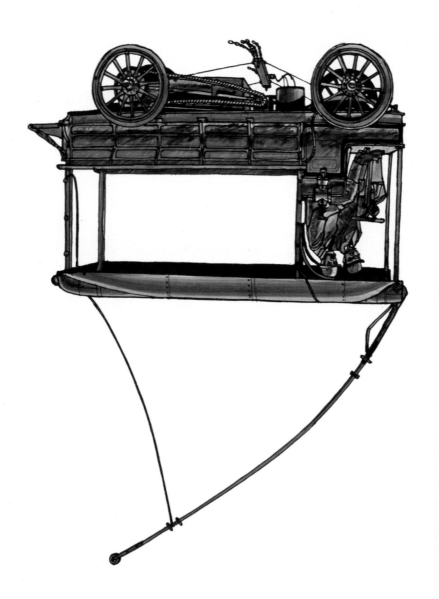

35

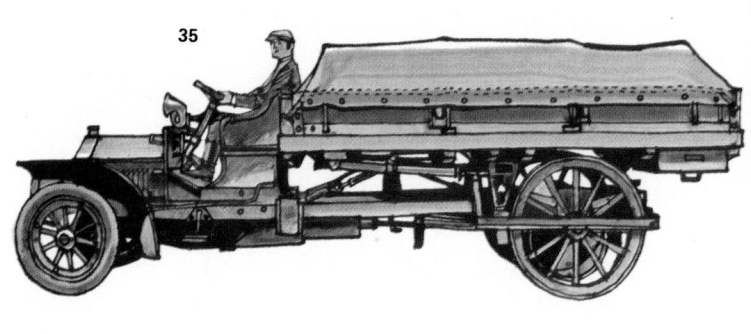

37

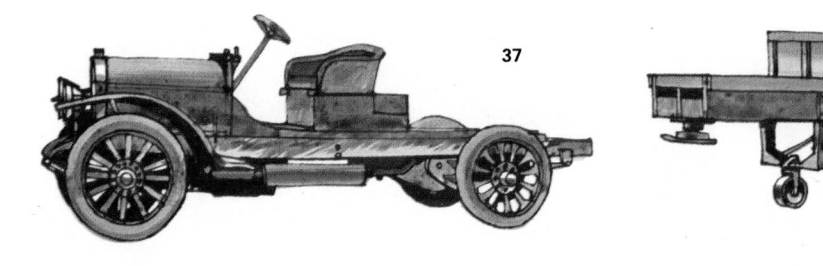

37/38

From Germany, Hansa-Automobil Gestell-schaft offered this 4-wheeled truck with 2-wheeled detachable body.

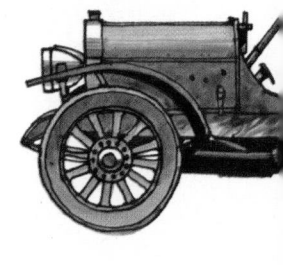

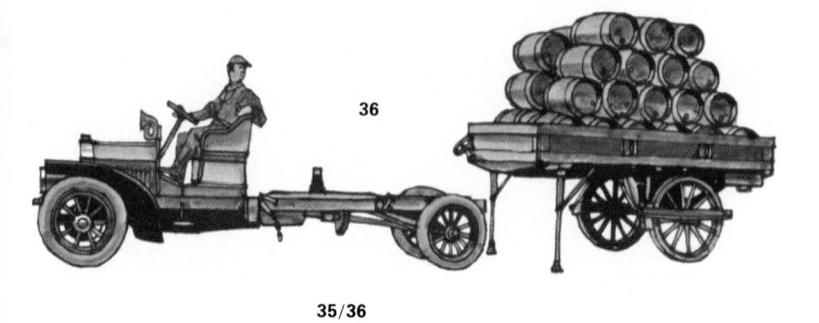

36

35/36

Though manufacturers and designers were slow to catch on, one advantage of the motor vehicle was that a motor did not have to stand idle, costing money, during loading and un-loading. When the idea did occur, there was a spate of offerings. From Belgium came the Auto-Mixte of Liege Pescatore system.

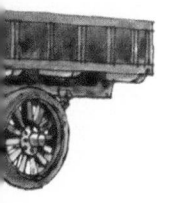

38

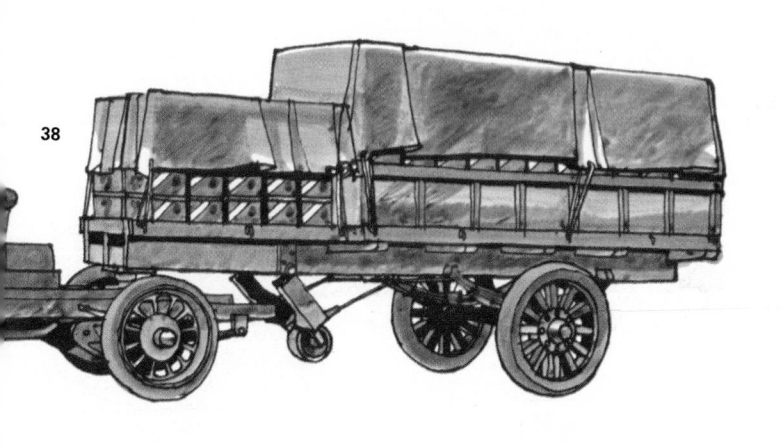

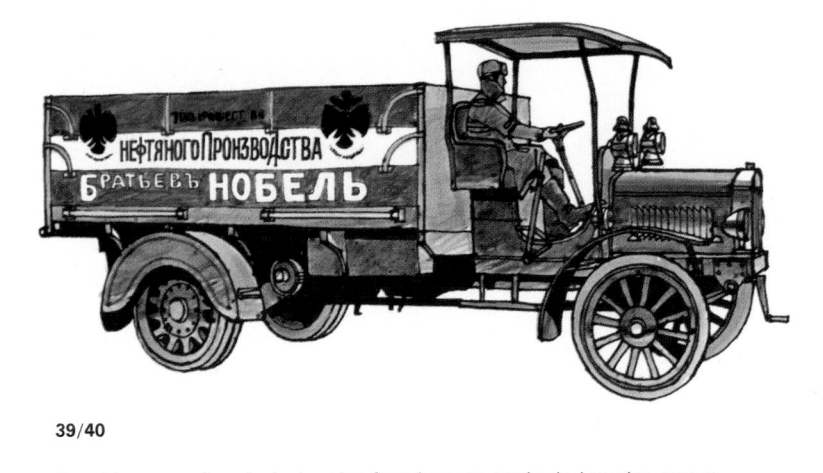

39/40

A problem many firms had, changing from horse to mechanical traction, was re-training the men. Most drivers, used to the leisurely ways of horse traffic, not only found the speed frightening, but changing gear a major difficulty. Electrics made life simpler for drivers but many firms producing petrol chassis had to offer easier gear changing. Commercial Cars of Luton designed their COMMER truck with a Linley pre-selective gearbox.

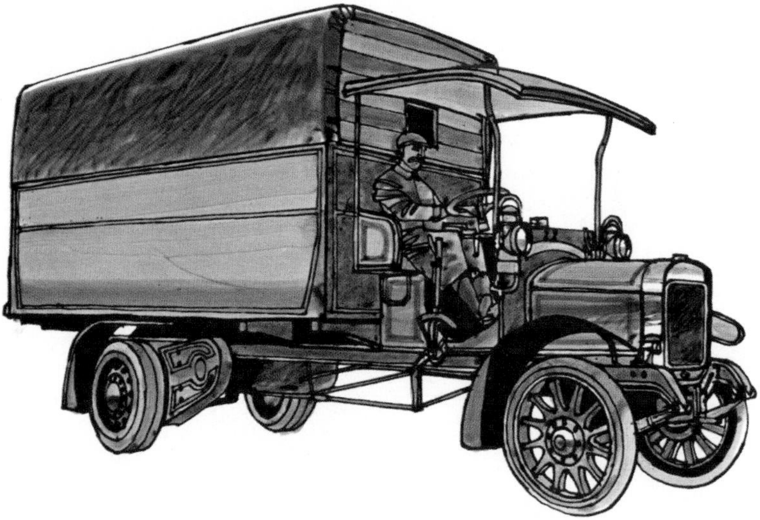

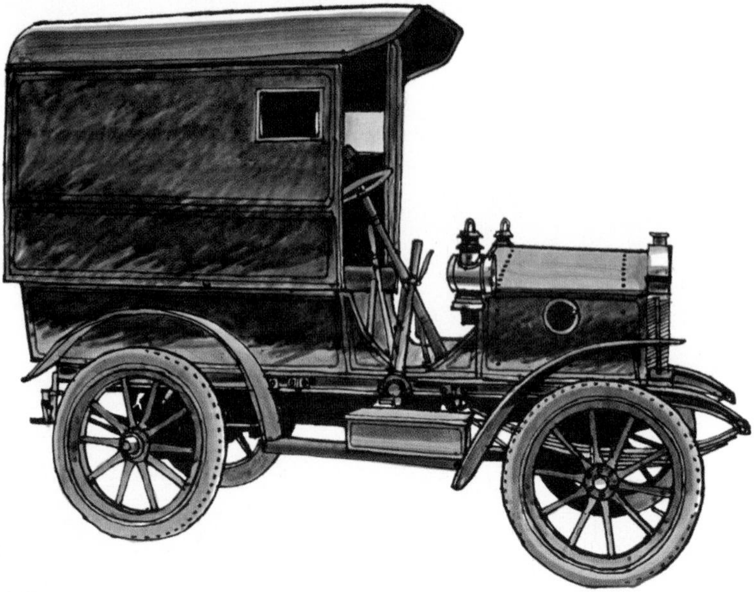

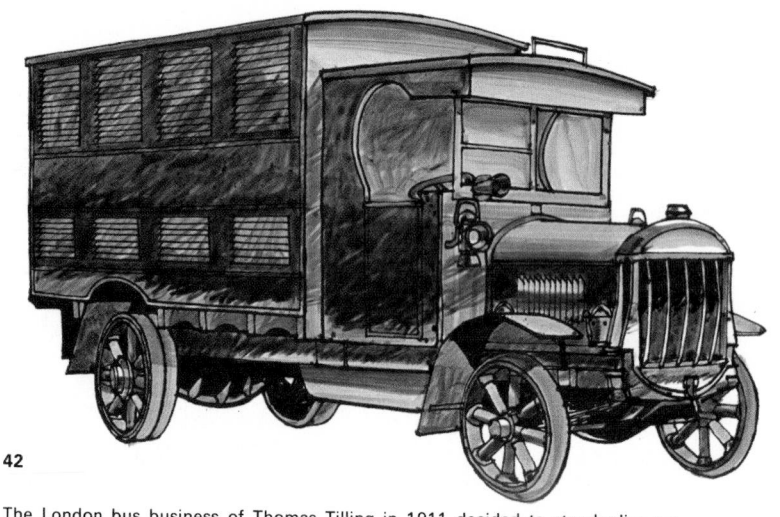

41

J. A. Wade of Liverpool, makers of the FORREST, thought they could overcome the problem with friction drive.

42

The London bus business of Thomas Tilling in 1911 decided to standardise on electric transmission after conclusive experiments made in conjunction with Mr W. A. Stevens. The Tilling Stevens name was eventually registered in 1915. The model shown here is a 1922 TS3.

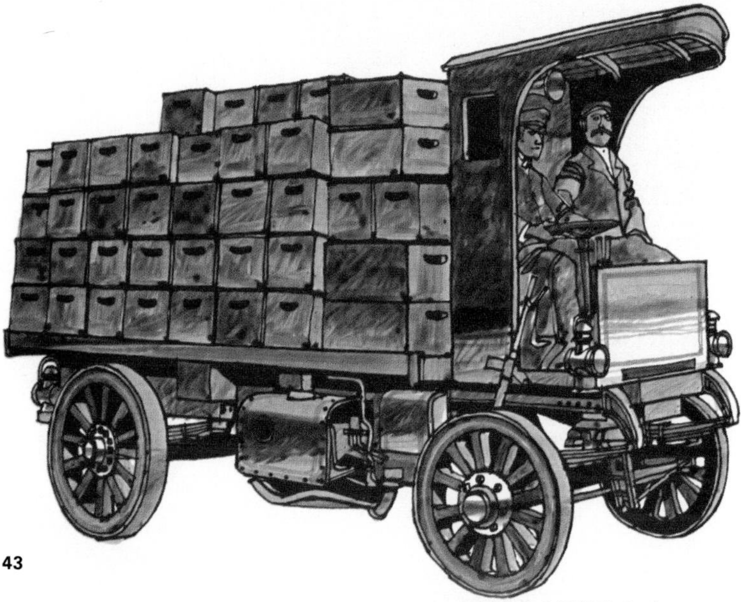

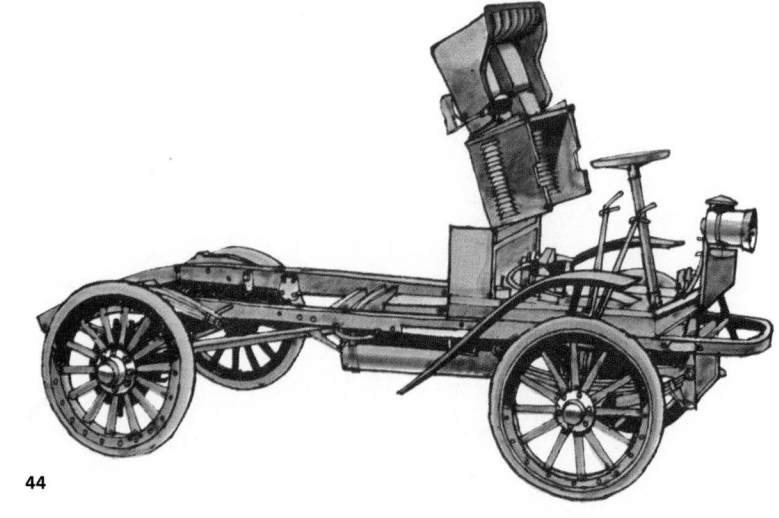

43

The low cost of fuel was the advantage offered by the BROOM & WADE single-cylinder paraffin truck. The manufacturers claimed the machine did 15,000 miles without an involuntary stop. These factors still failed to attract enough purchasers.

44

The cab over the engine design favoured in the States was the exception rather than the rule in Britain. The engine accessibility afforded by this *c.* 1909 AUTOCAR is something today's manufacturers could learn from. The engine and transmission were mounted on a sub-frame for quick and easy replacement.

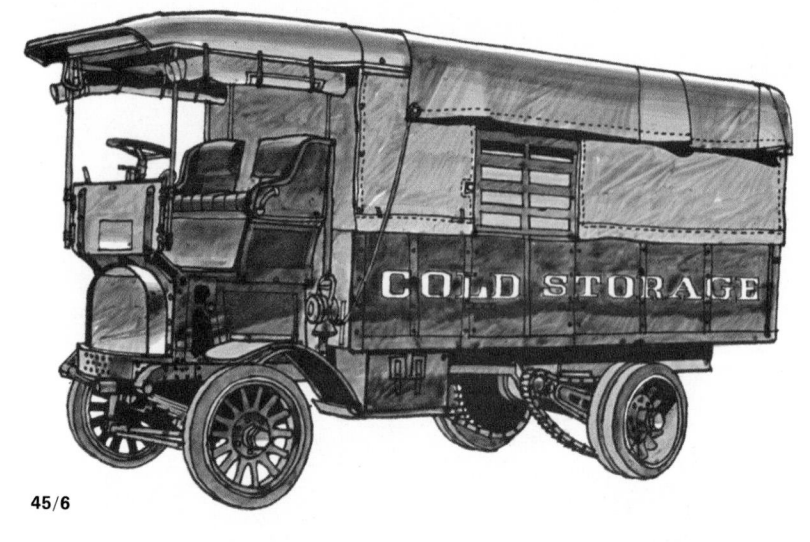

45/6

Whilst many early manufacturers offering trucks in the States had difficulty establishing their products and remaining in business, Mack Brothers were so successful that they had to move to larger premises at Allentown, Pa in 1904. These two are typical 3—5 ton cab-over-engine MANHATTANS made by Mack Bros between 1905 and 1911.

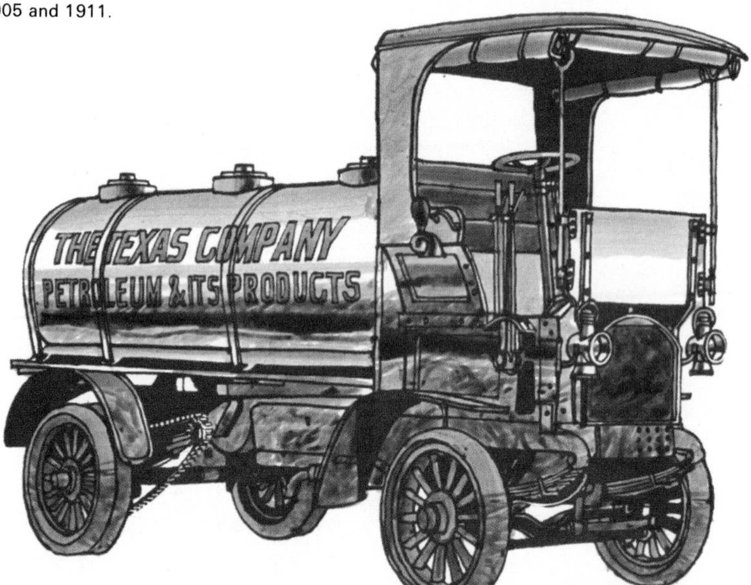

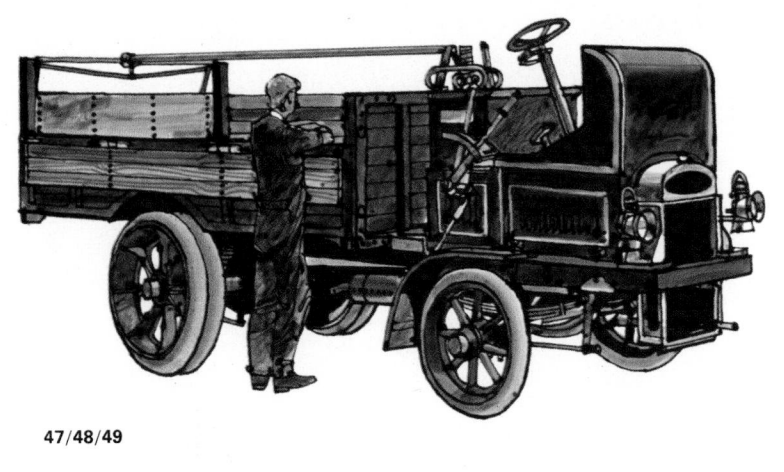

47/48/49

One of the first British firms to try the cab-over-engine design was the Lancashire Steam Motor Co (Leyland). The design was pioneered in 1905 without too much success, but by 1909, having acquired the nickname 'Pig', this line of Model Ys was selling in reasonable numbers.

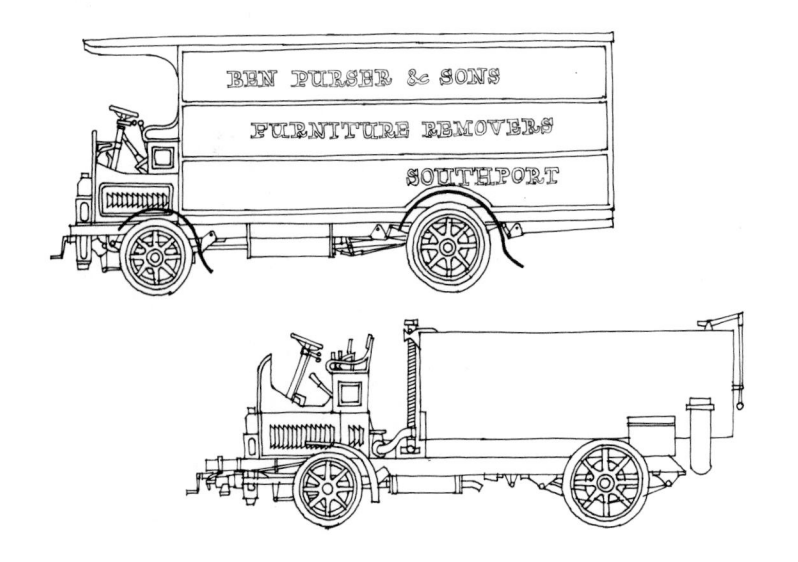

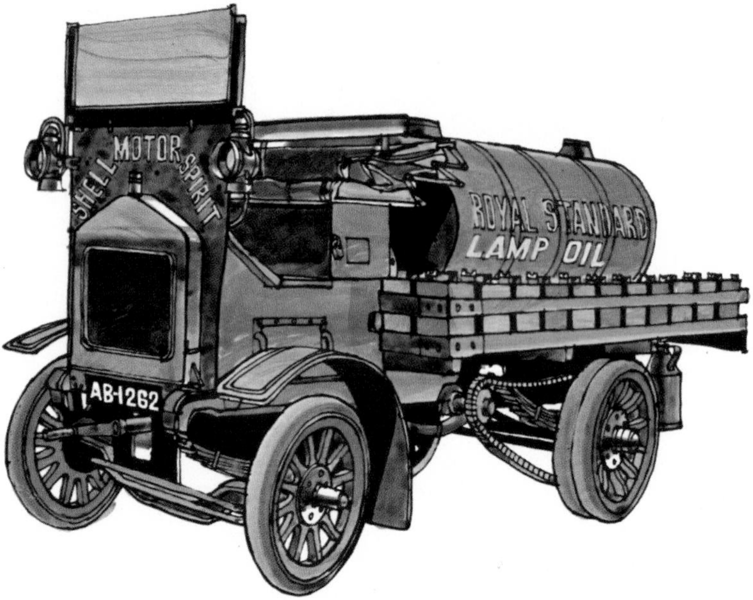

50/51

The Karrier truck earned its initial reputation for reliability and ease of driving in and around the very hilly parts of Yorkshire.

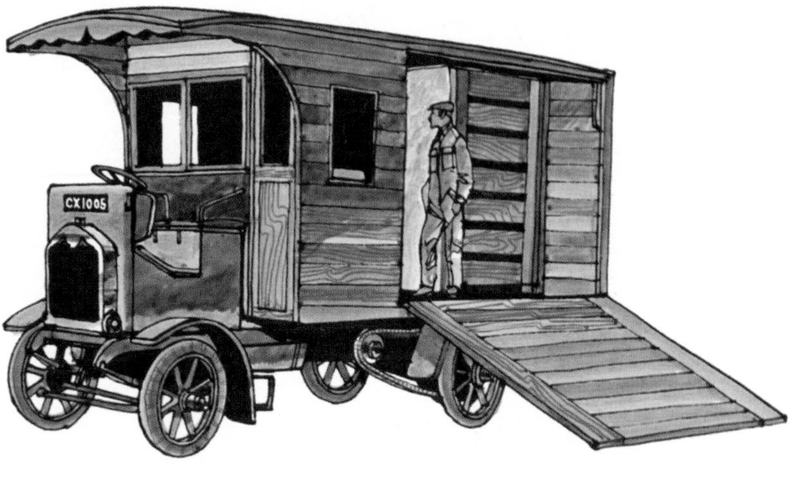

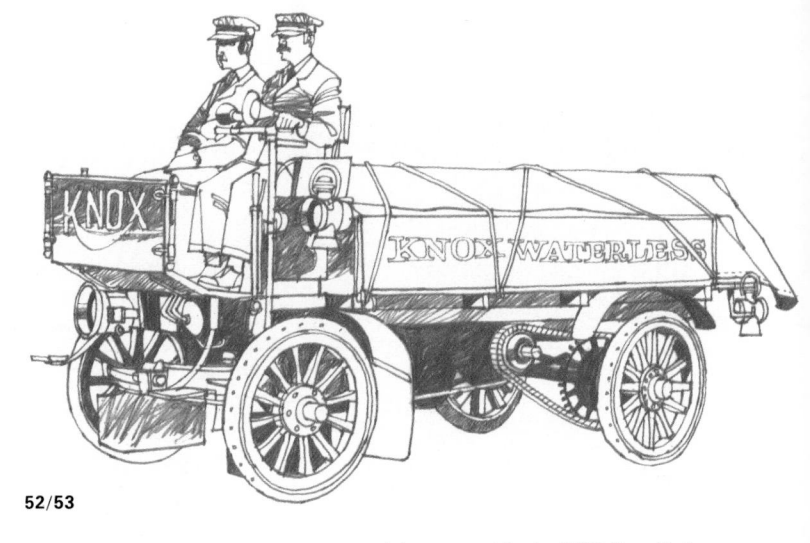

52/53

The Knox Waterless was the most successful contestant in the 1903 New York Truck Contest. Knox afterwards became a marque particularly respected by truckers, remaining successful until the First World War. Instead of a normal cooling system, Knox employed air cooling by means of corrugated pins which gave each cylinder the look of a porcupine.

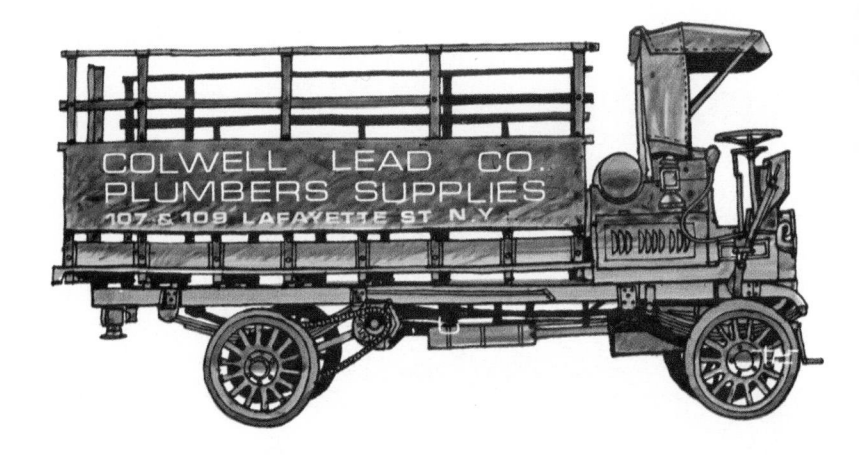

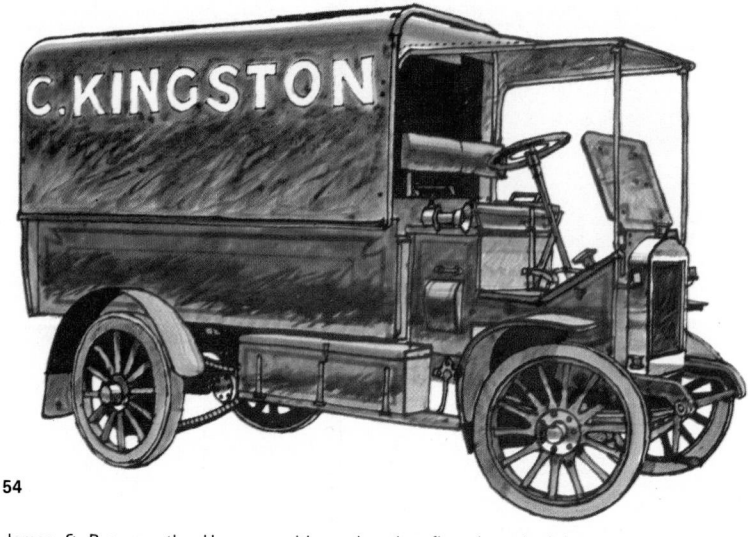

54

James & Browne, the Hammersmith engineering firm, later had Lacre Lorries market their range under the trade name 'J. B. Lacre'.

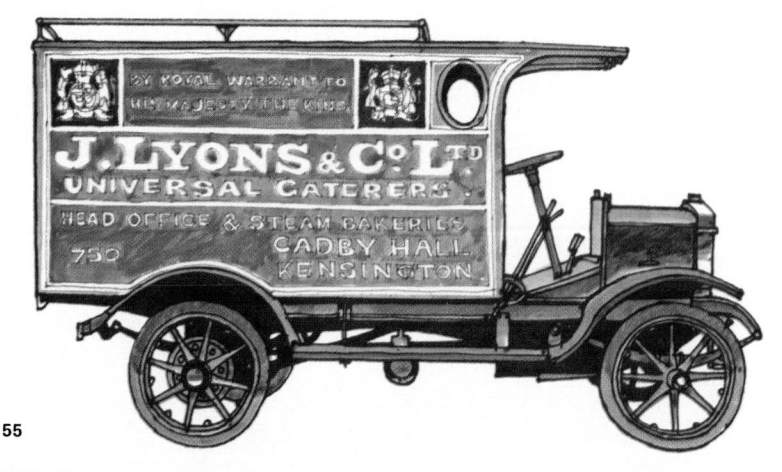

55

1911 15-cwt van made by STRAKER & SQUIRE. Sydney Straker had many partnerships in the automobile industry from before the turn of the century and in his life promoted everything in the vehicle spectrum from steam wagons to petrol trams.

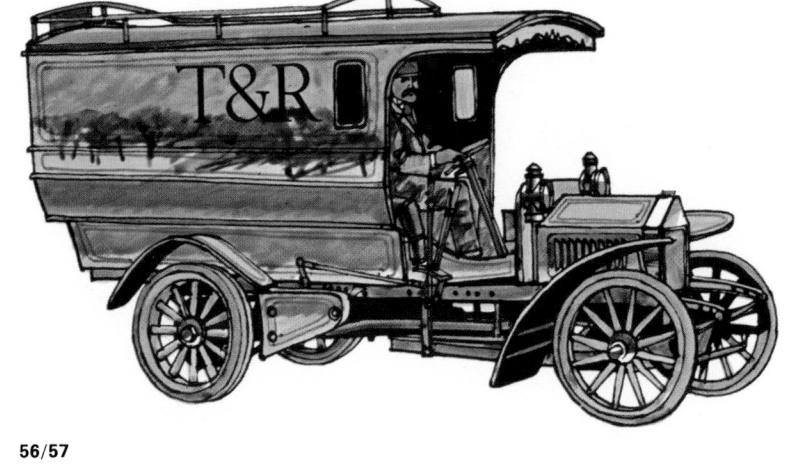

56/57

A popular make of light van in the South of England before the First World War was the LACRE. The company later became renowned for its concentration in the municipal field—producing road sweepers, cleansing equipment, etc.

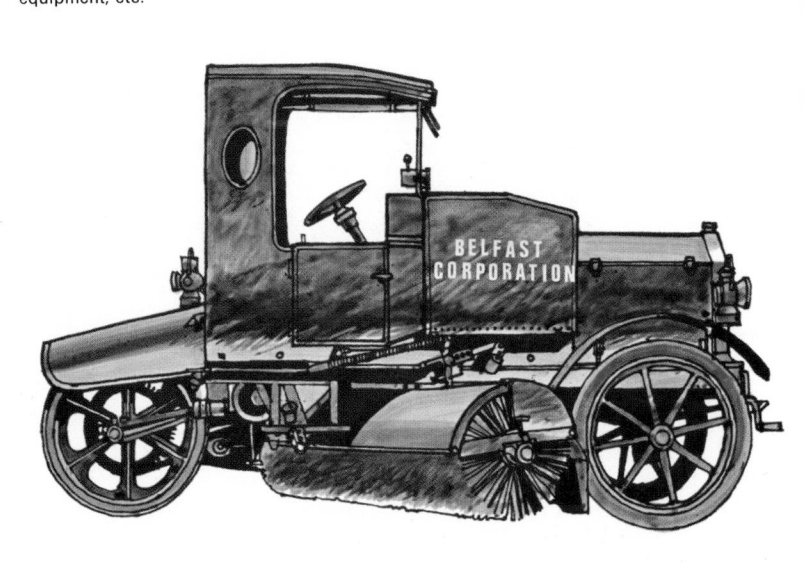

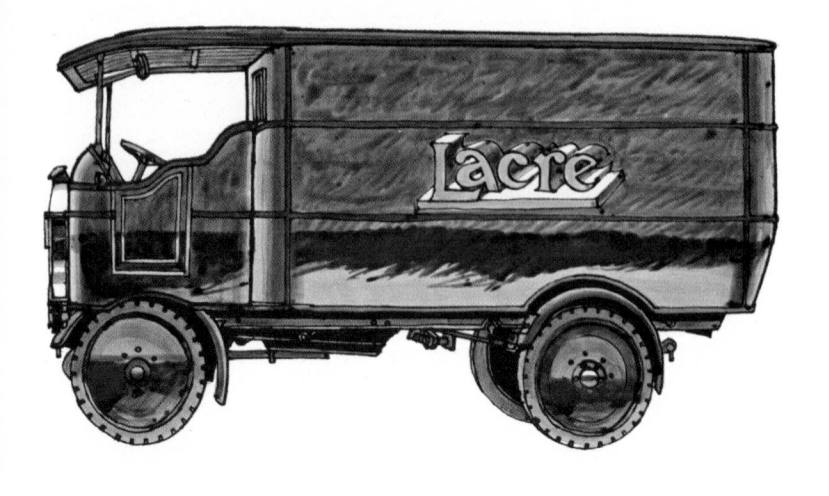

58/59

1911 saw LACRE announce this model. It offered an engine that could be wheeled out for very quick maintenance or change; here there was no need to 'get out and get under'. The idea was pioneered in the States by Max Grabowsky, whose popular line of trucks was to become part of General Motors. Today, London Transport's Routemaster buses use the same technique.

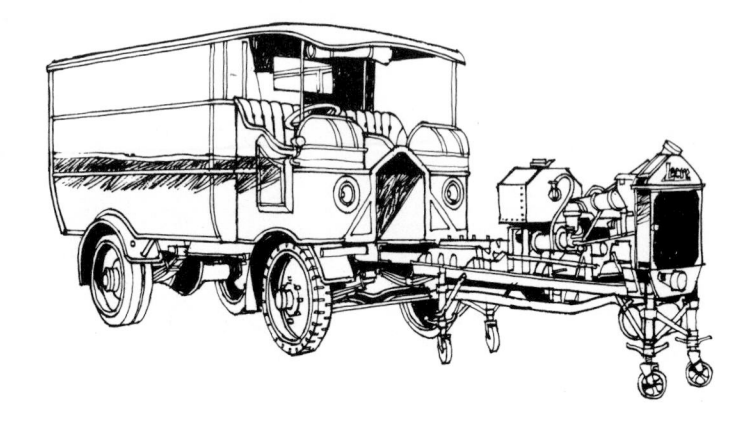

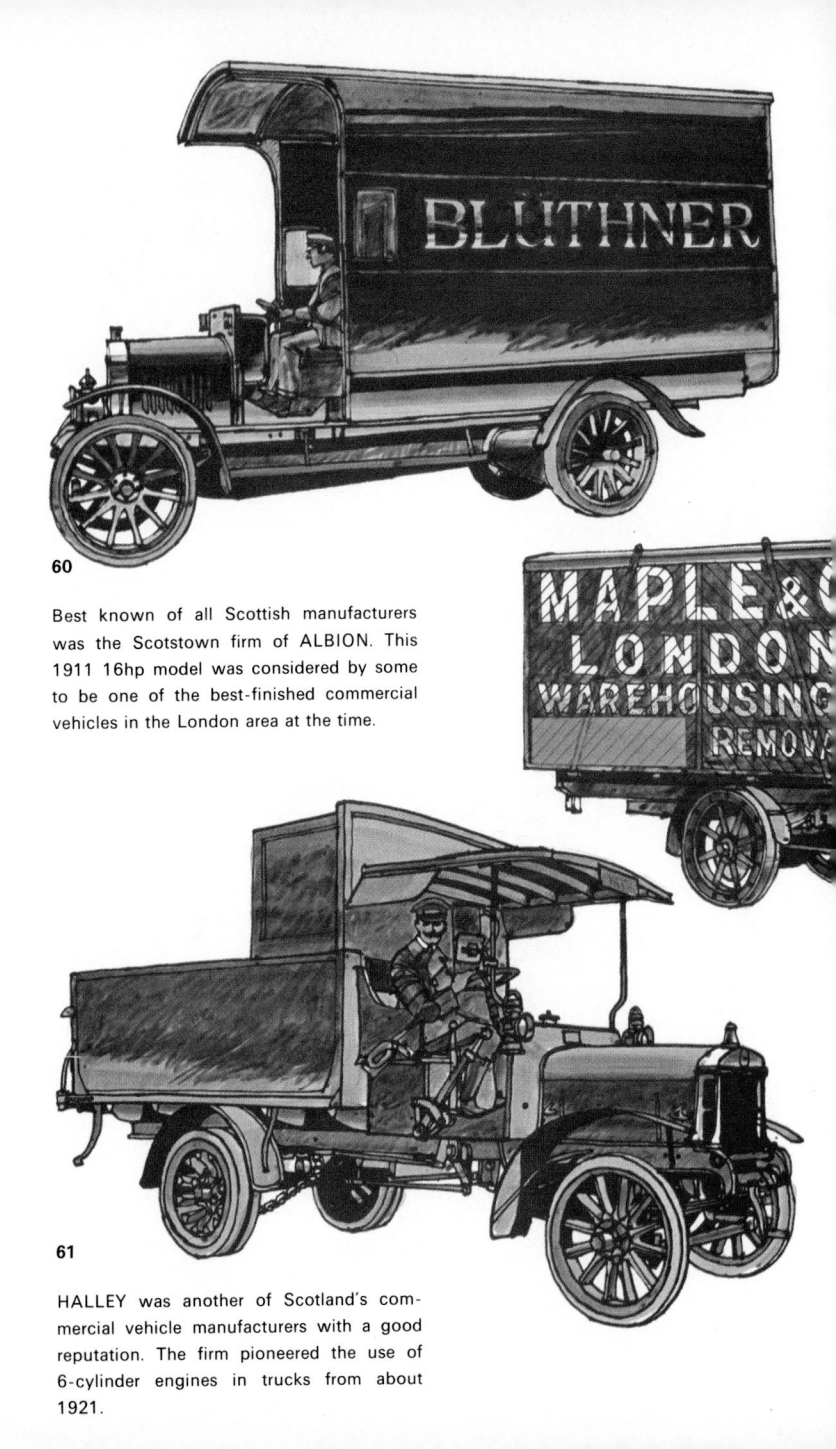

60

Best known of all Scottish manufacturers was the Scotstown firm of ALBION. This 1911 16hp model was considered by some to be one of the best-finished commercial vehicles in the London area at the time.

61

HALLEY was another of Scotland's commercial vehicle manufacturers with a good reputation. The firm pioneered the use of 6-cylinder engines in trucks from about 1921.

62

Today we call this containerisation. In 1908,
before firms trusted sending their vehicles
to Europe, one simply took the lift van to
the nearest railway yard.

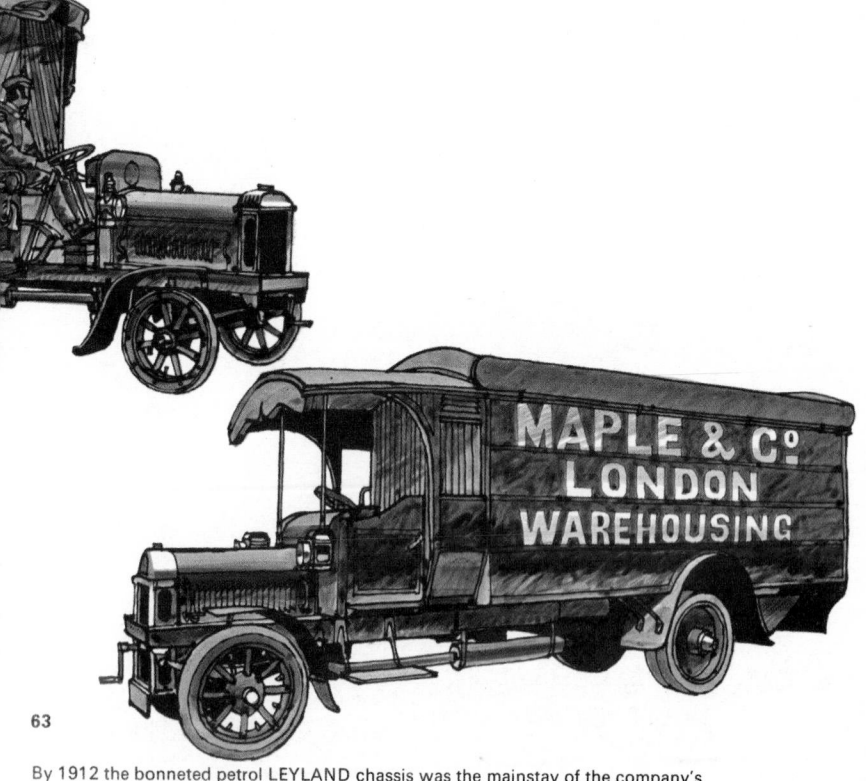

By 1912 the bonneted petrol LEYLAND chassis was the mainstay of the company's
production. Sales of the 'Pig' were limited to those requiring a short-chassis job.
These massive pantechnicons were greatly used by the big London stores—
many purchased through the Government's £120 subsidy scheme.

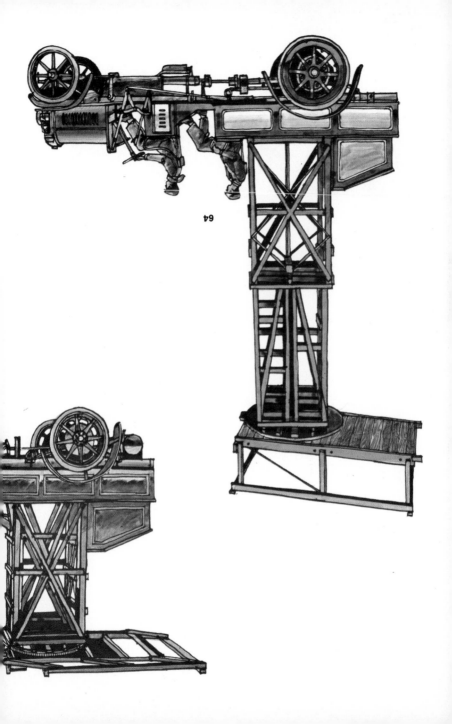

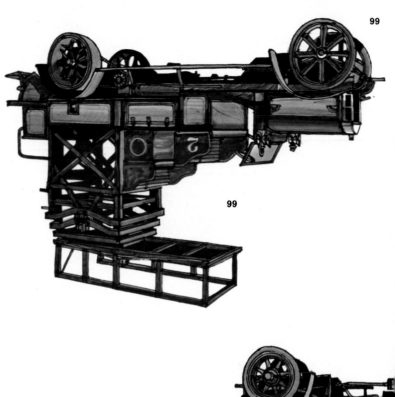

64/65

The period before the First World War was really the heyday of the tramcar. Overhead wiring needed constant attention and LEYLAND found a ready market for both screw and rope action tower wagons.

66

What a marvellous position afforded to the crew sitting in the rear seat of this 1911 ALBION tower wagon.

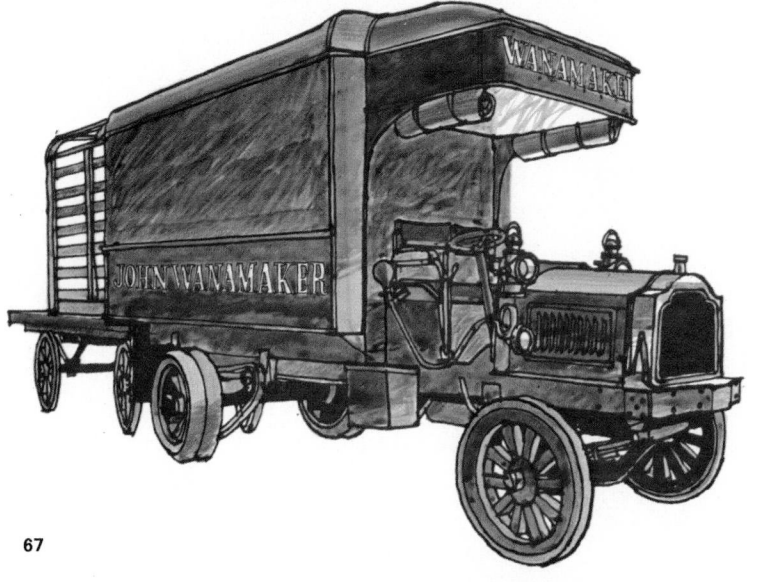

67

When the high-class American car manufacturer, PACKARD, introduced their truck range in 1909, they opted for the British/European trend of putting the engine in front of the driver—the idea changed the whole concept of the American truck in five years. This Packard for Wanamaker is novel in having a sleeved container body for quick turnaround.

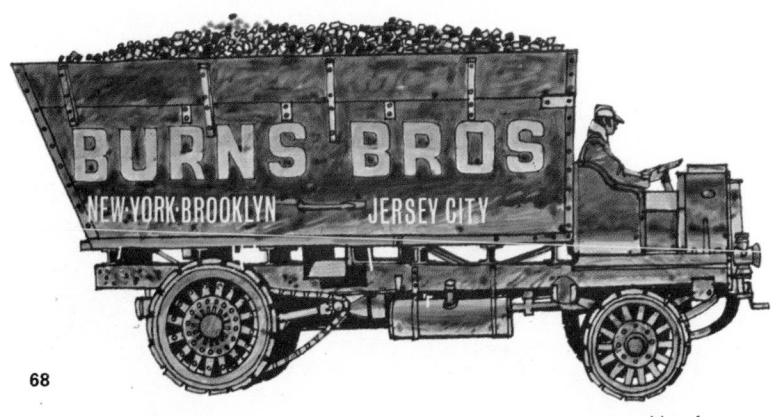

68

First petrol-engined truck to achieve commercial success that was capable of carrying a 10-ton load was the HEWITT, made in New York. The problem of carrying such a load was not finding a suitable motor, but tyres. The Hewitt overcame the problem with a tyre formed of heavy rubber blocks—a tyre for which Kelly-Springfield became famed.

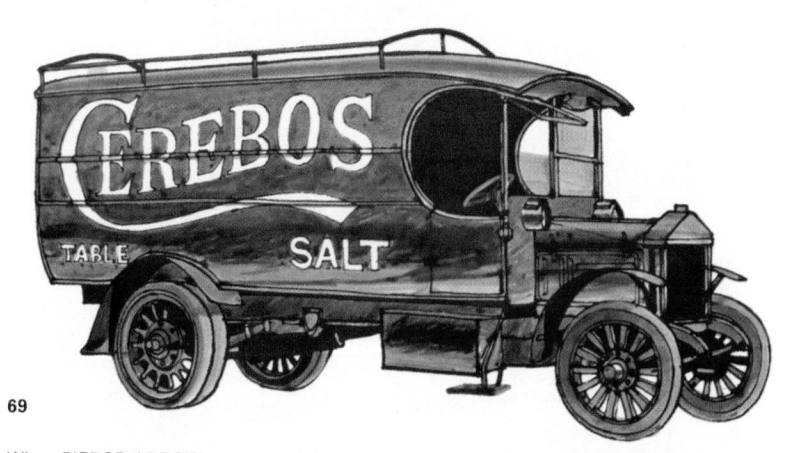

69

When PIERCE-ARROW announced their truck chassis in 1911 it set a new trend in America for the European-inspired shaft drive. The Pierce-Arrow truck was such a good design for that year that the manufacturers never revised the model for 14 years—by which time, although still a good truck, it had sadly become an anachronism.

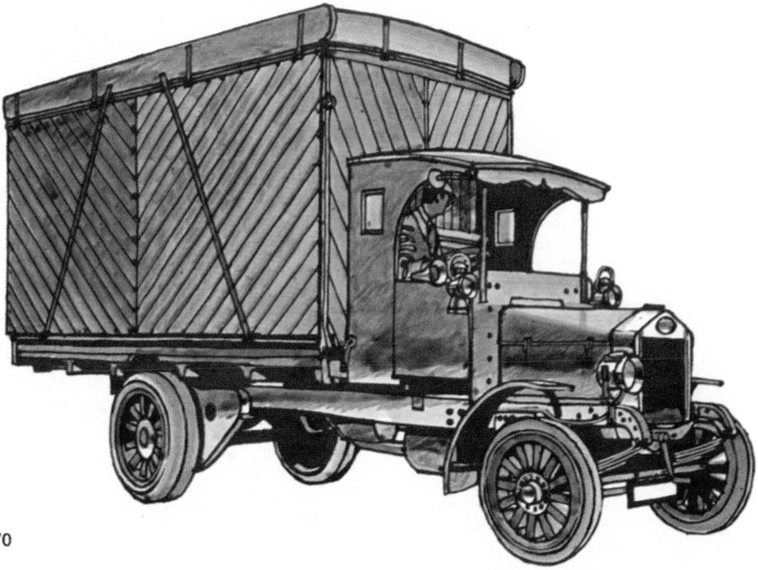

70

Chain drive died slowly. US manufacturers were never truly convinced of the worm drive for heavy loads until well after the Great War. In Britain HALLFORD were the only notable firm to cling to chains until the early twenties.

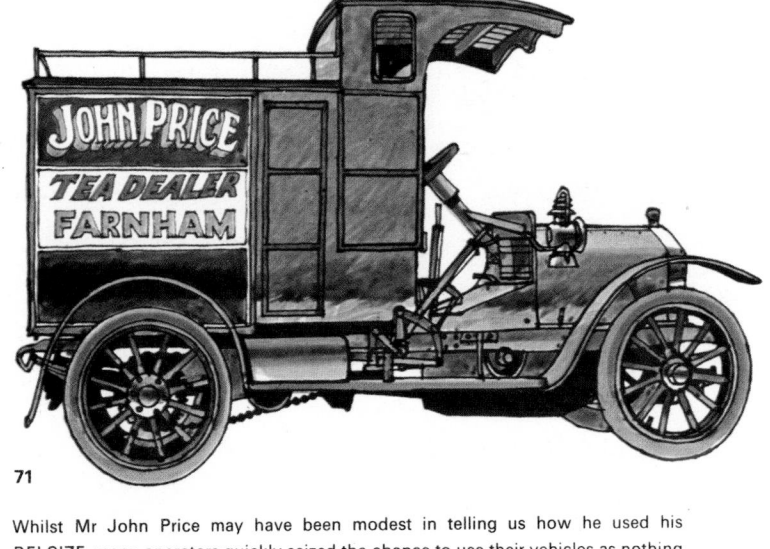

71

Whilst Mr John Price may have been modest in telling us how he used his BELSIZE, many operators quickly seized the chance to use their vehicles as nothing more than ornamental displays.

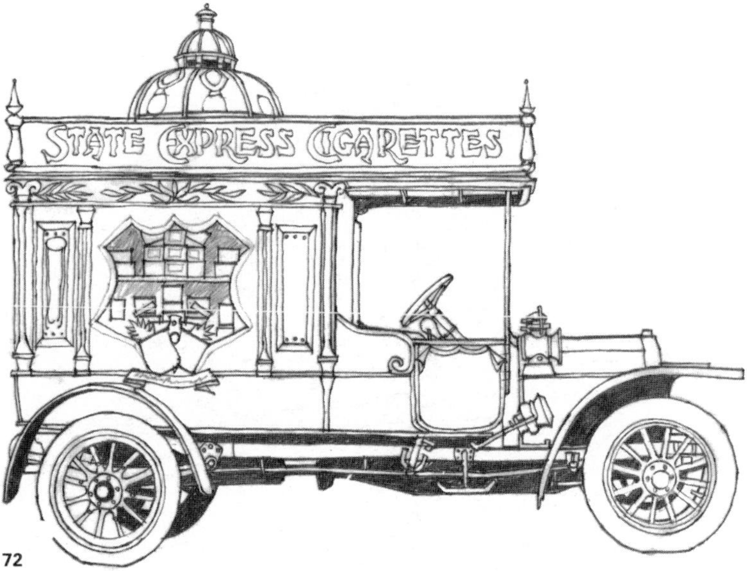

72

State Express no doubt did make the odd delivery in their 1907 DENNIS.

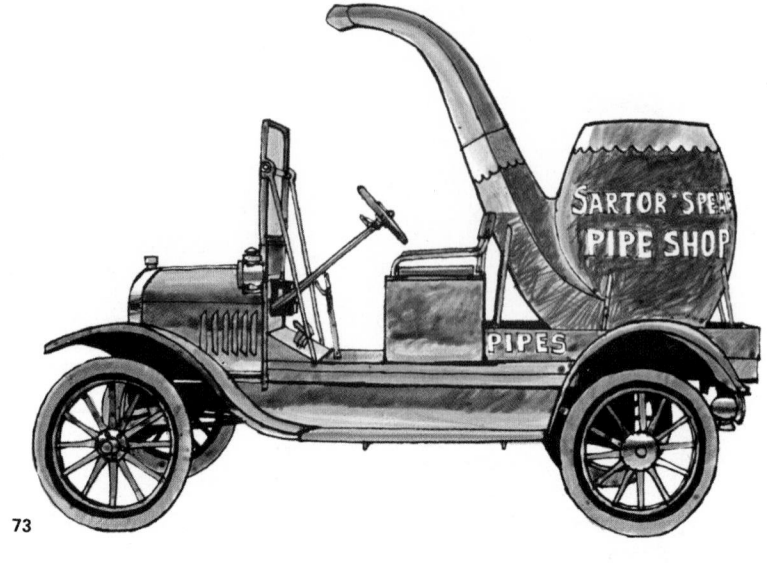

73

. . . but did the pipe shop do anything with their 1921 FORD MODEL T except take it to fetes?

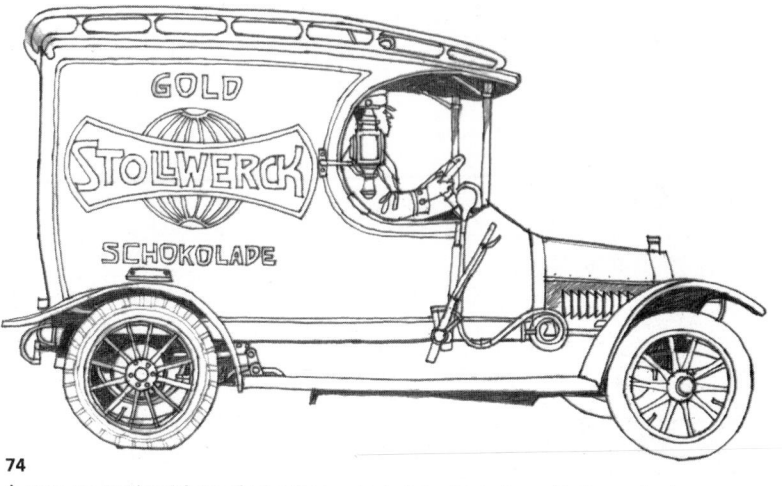

74

A more conventional form of advertising which did not interfere with the payload space. This particular N. A. G. used by Stollwerck chocolate was considered at the time to be extremely dignified.

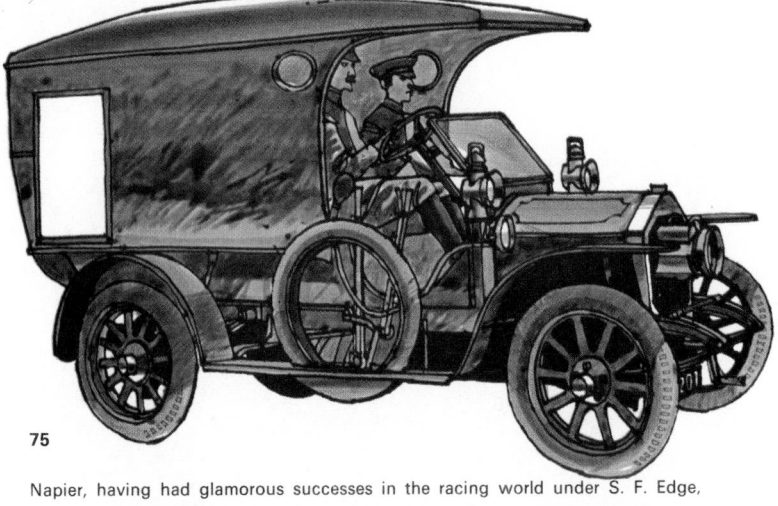

75

Napier, having had glamorous successes in the racing world under S. F. Edge, supplemented their range of high-class cars with a light commercial chassis, more often than not seen supporting a taxicab body.

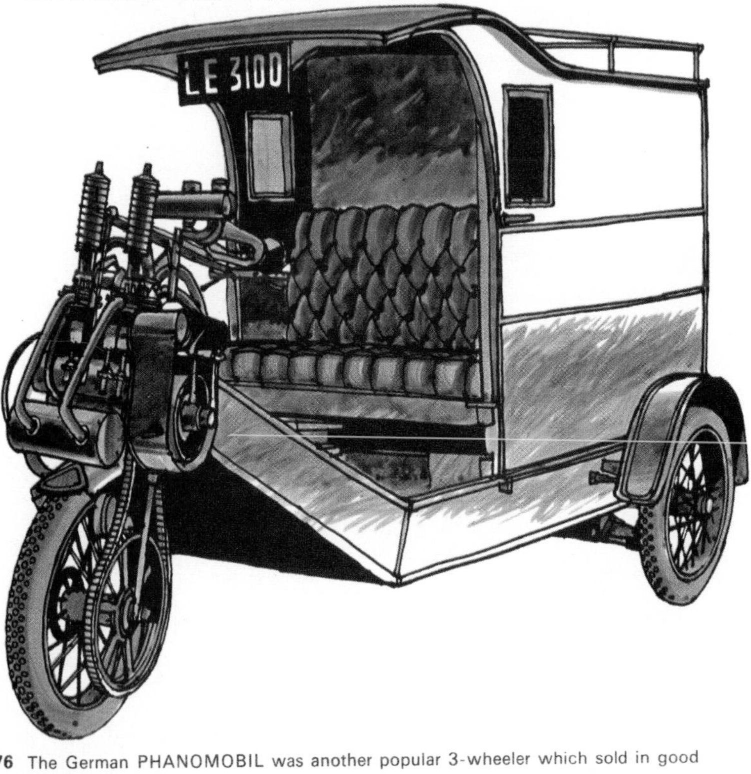

76 The German PHANOMOBIL was another popular 3-wheeler which sold in good numbers over many years.

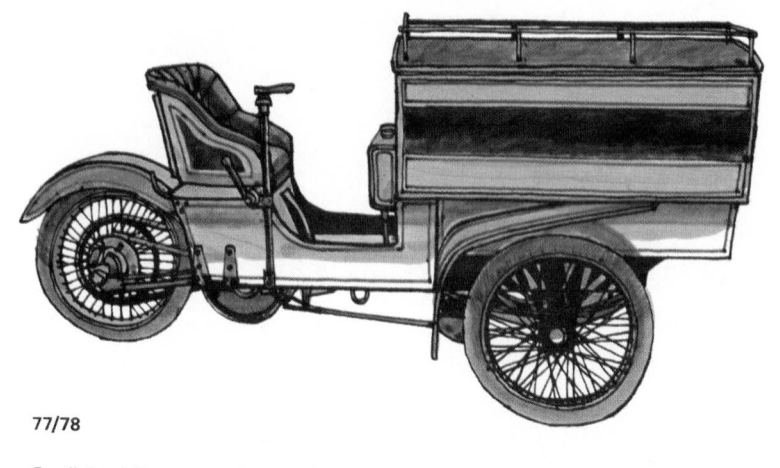

77/78

For light delivery around town the British and Europeans opted for the cycle carrier. To the forefront of the cycle carrier market were Autocarriers; this small South London business of Weller and Portwine blossomed forth to become AC Cars at Thames Ditton.

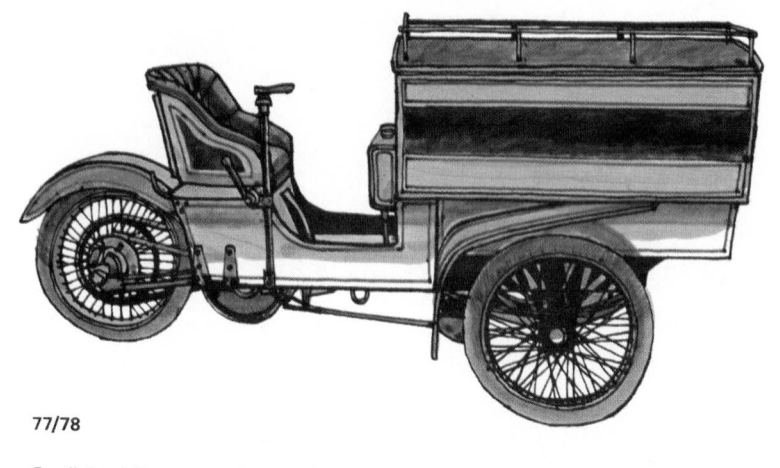

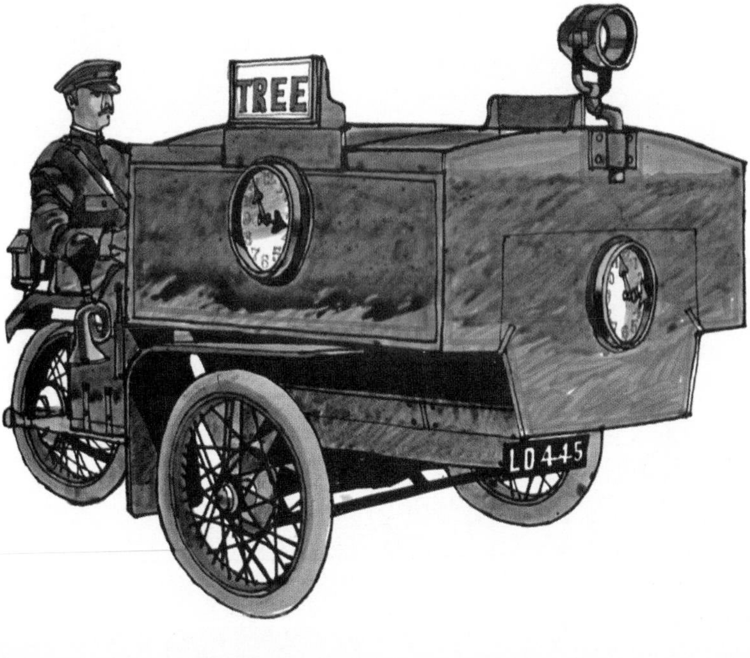

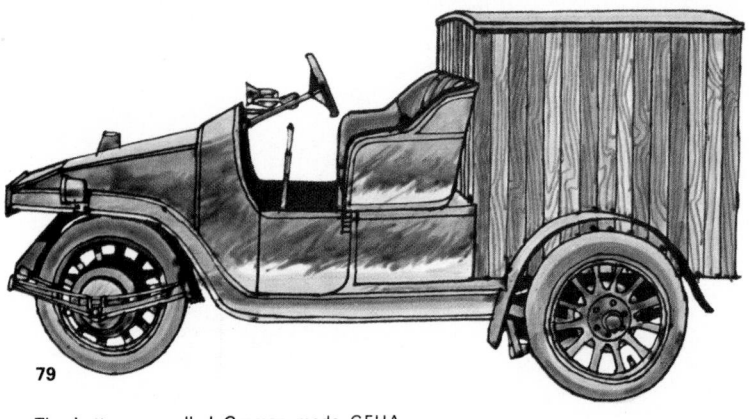

79

The battery-propelled German-made GEHA
had not the same popularity as the PHANO-
MOBIL.

80

Nor did the British GIRLING which was made
in Bedford just prior to the Great War.

81

Special bodies for municipal corporations is
another market which has grown over the
years into a highly specialised business. The
clearing of drains demanded a highly compli-
cated-looking body, termed a gully-emptier.

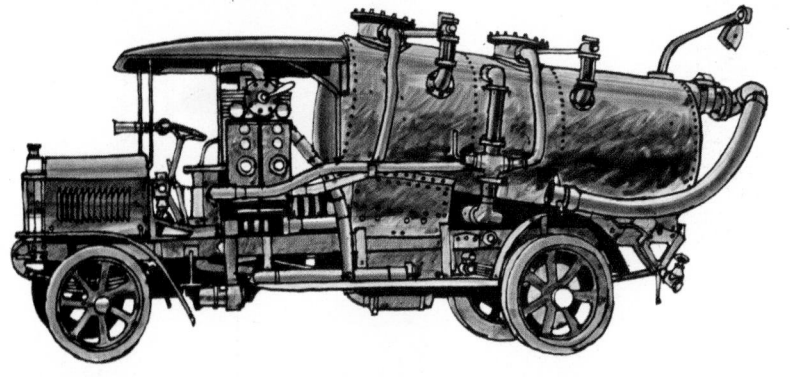

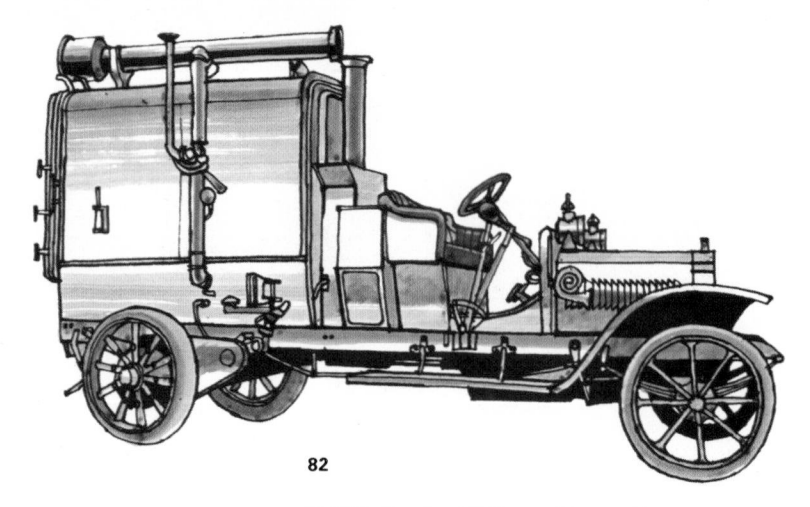

82

In 1911 Dresden felt the need to provide a disinfecting service which prodded BENZ into offering their chassis with a self-propelled steam disinfecting chamber.

80

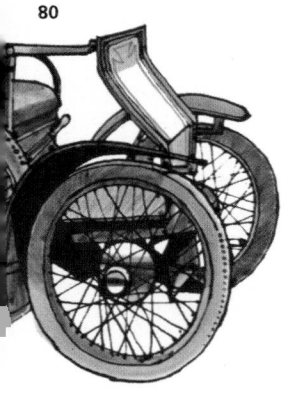

83

Vienna Corporation in the same year arranged with Messrs PUCH (a division of Austro-Daimler) to have a water sprinkler that could also act as a fire engine. Vienna Municipality claimed it could send a jet over their Town Hall.

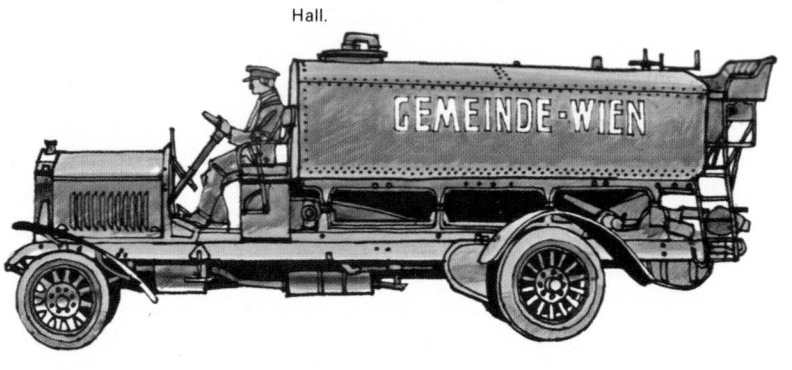

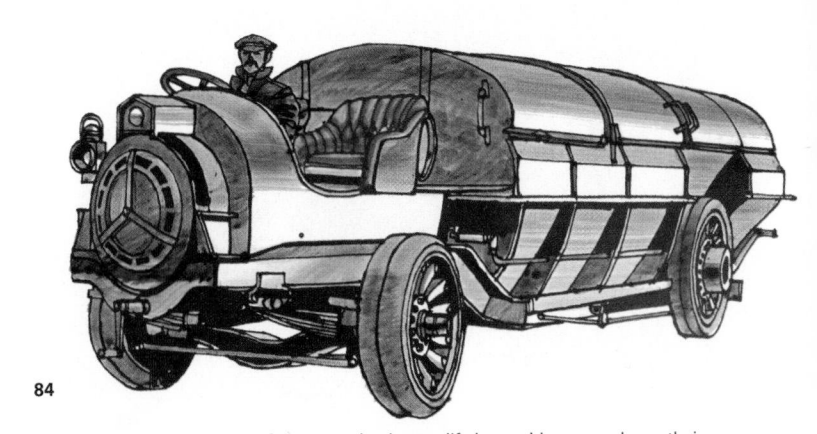

84

To overcome the problem of dustmen having to lift heavy bins way above their heads, DE DION-BOUTON designed this four-wheel drive dropped-frame chassis in 1911. Is this the world's first dropped chassis?

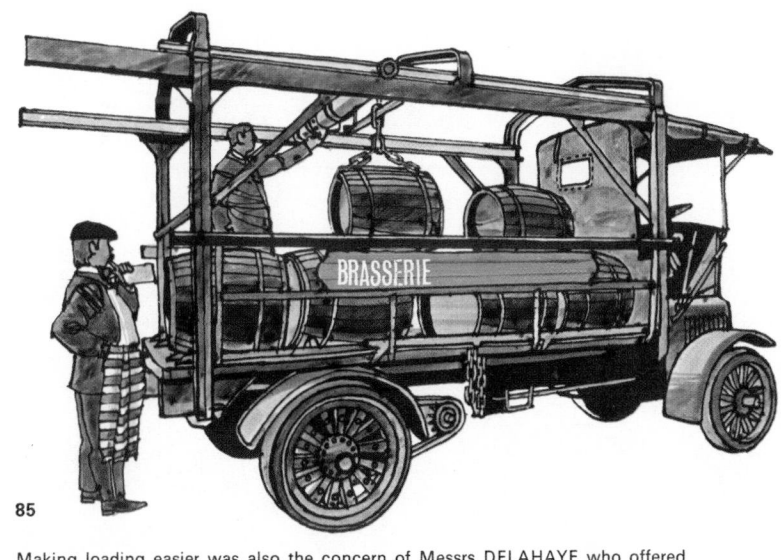

85

Making loading easier was also the concern of Messrs DELAHAYE who offered electric hoisting and tracking gear, probably to brewers, who could no doubt do with such an innovation today considering the noise made by brewery men.

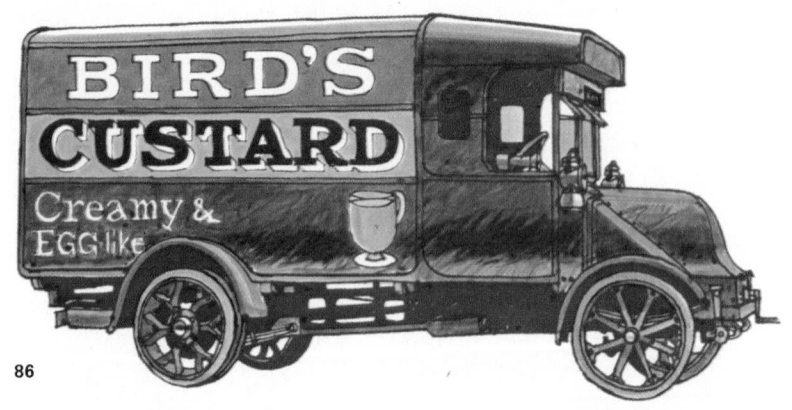

86

AUSTIN'S venture into the heavy goods market produced a unique chassis.
Among its outstanding features was a propeller shaft driving each rear wheel via
separate crown wheels and a centrally mounted gear stick.

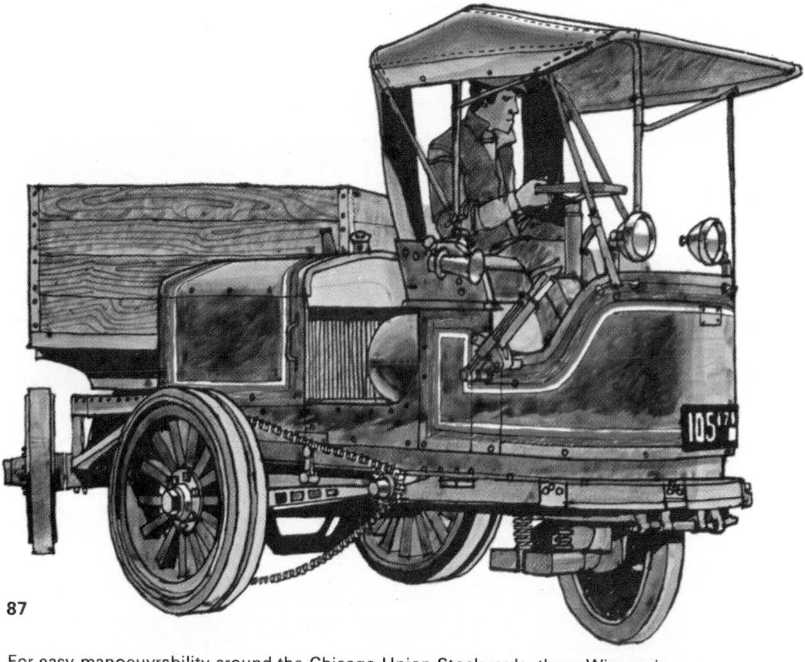

87

For easy manoeuvrability around the Chicago Union Stockyards, these Wisconsin-
engined mechanical horses were built to the design of G. W. Bulley.

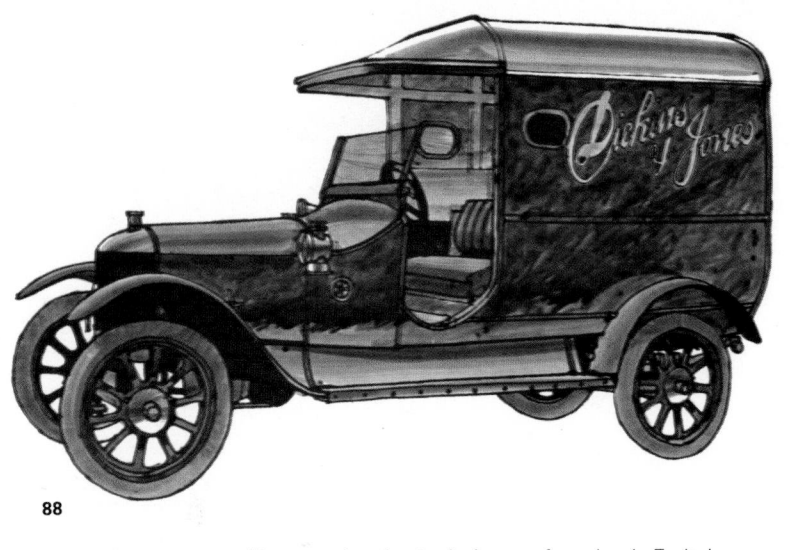

88

Many light vans were nothing more than the standard range of car chassis. Typical is this A. C. which had the gearbox in-unit with the axle. This avoided having full torque of the engine and transmission transferring weight from one wheel to another precipitating wheelspin.

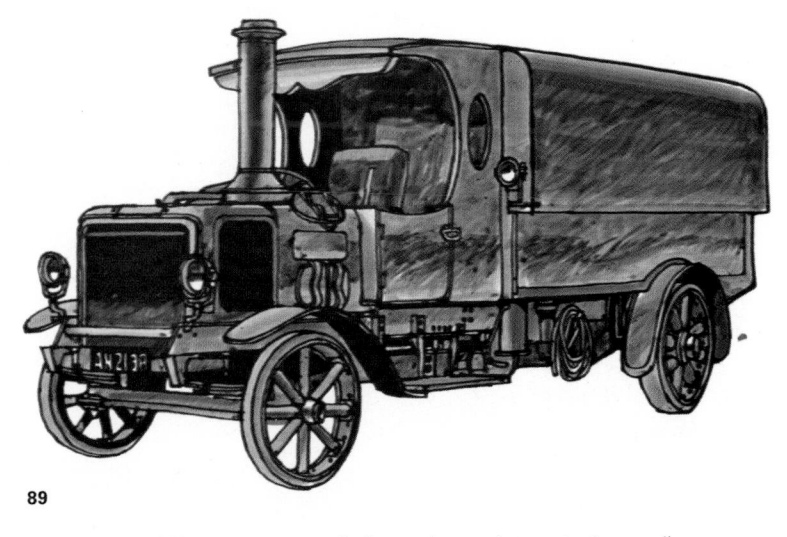

89

Thomas CLARKSON, a steam man to the last, a pioneer of steam trucks as well as a London steam bus operator, tried to exploit the wartime market with his coke and paraffin-fired lorries built on chassis similar to his buses.

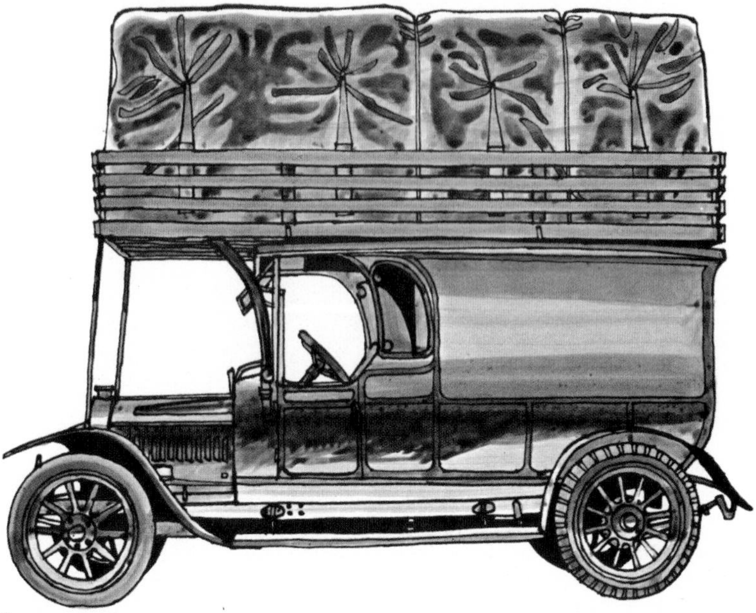

90

No sooner had the Great War begun than the clamour for home-produced fuel started. Gas containers and conversions were plentiful.

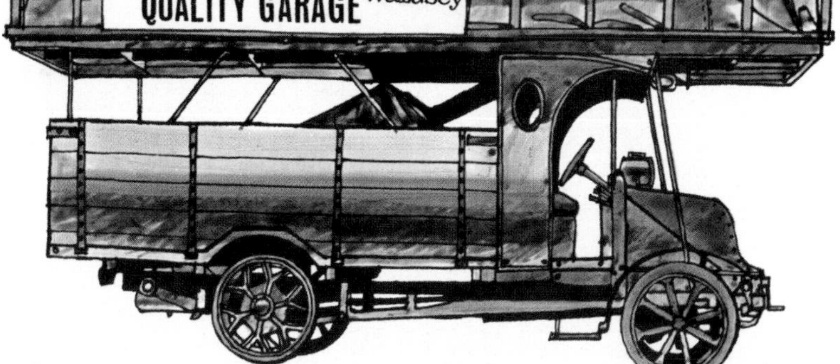

LIVERPOOL TO LONDON BY GAS.
QUALITY GARAGE wallasey

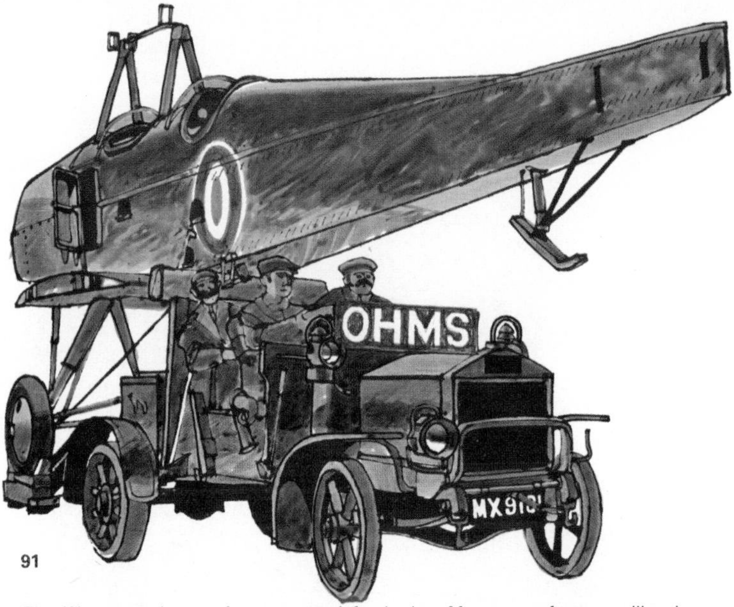

91

The War created an unforeseen need for lorries. Many manufacturers, like the American FWD, were saved from insolvency by its demands. NAPIER turned over their entire factory to the war effort. Napiers, like Leylands, Thornycrofts and AECs, became impossible to buy on the home market.

92 This created an influx of American chassis at astronomical prices, and firms at home like CALEDON, formerly Scottish Commercial Cars, whose chassis was not licensed under the subsidy scheme, tried very hard for their slice of the home market.

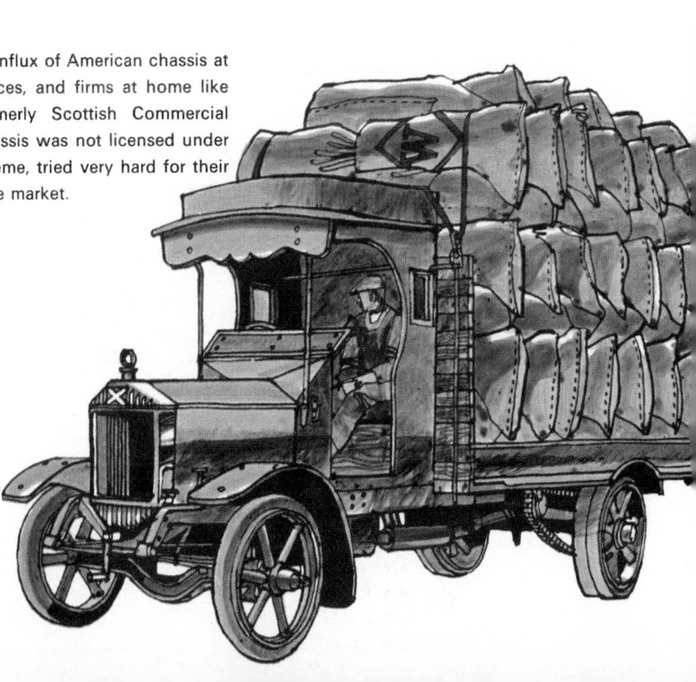

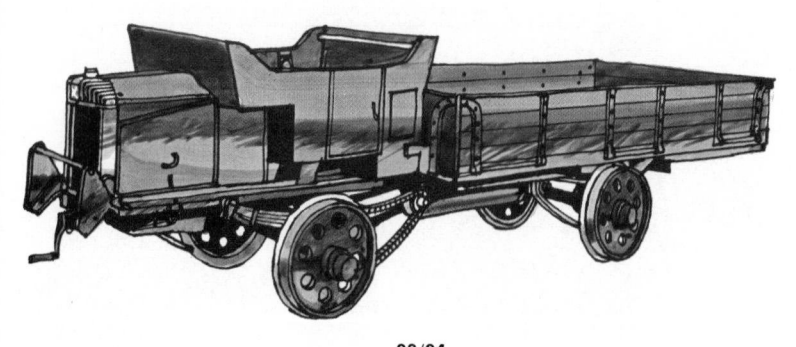

93/94

Six CALEDON chassis were sent to Aldershot, some offered as petrol rail cars for consideration by the military. All were returned after a few weeks to the manufacturers. The Caledon chassis was beset with transmission problems over the years, giving untold trouble to their purchasers. Caledon's public relations more than excelled themselves, giving the impression that thousands were built, whereas the number barely reached three figures.

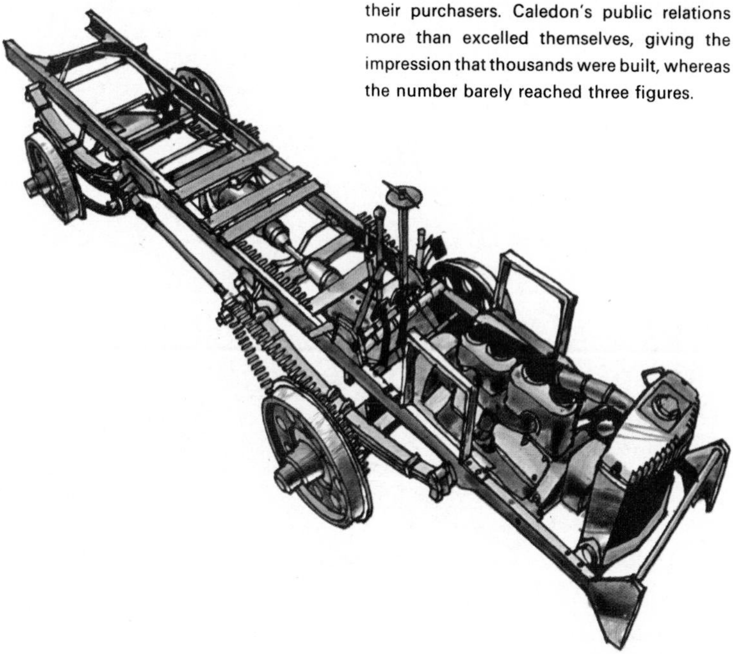

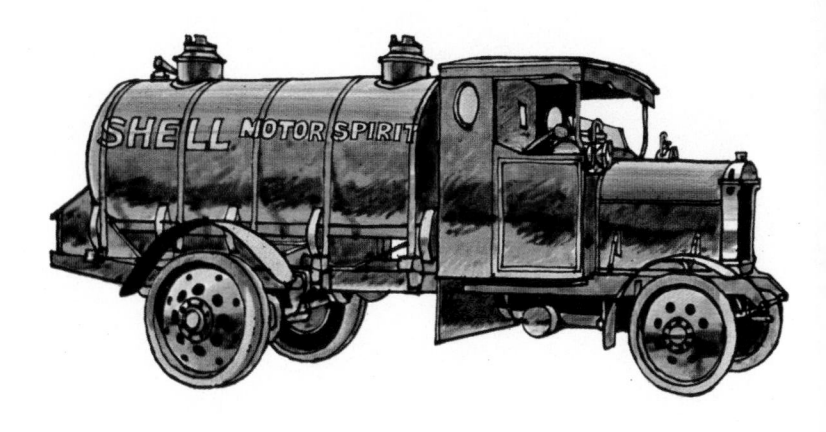

95/6

When the war ended, trucks by the thousands, of all countries, were sold off at government auctions. Some manufacturers chose to try and buy back what they could so as not to have their postwar markets ruined. Manufacturers reconditioned and sold them over a number of years under guarantee. These two THORNYCROFT Js show new and reconditioned subsidy types (with disc wheels) sold side by side in 1921.

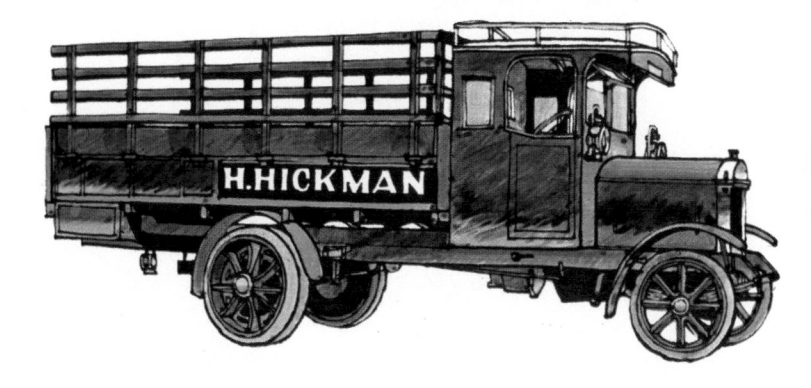

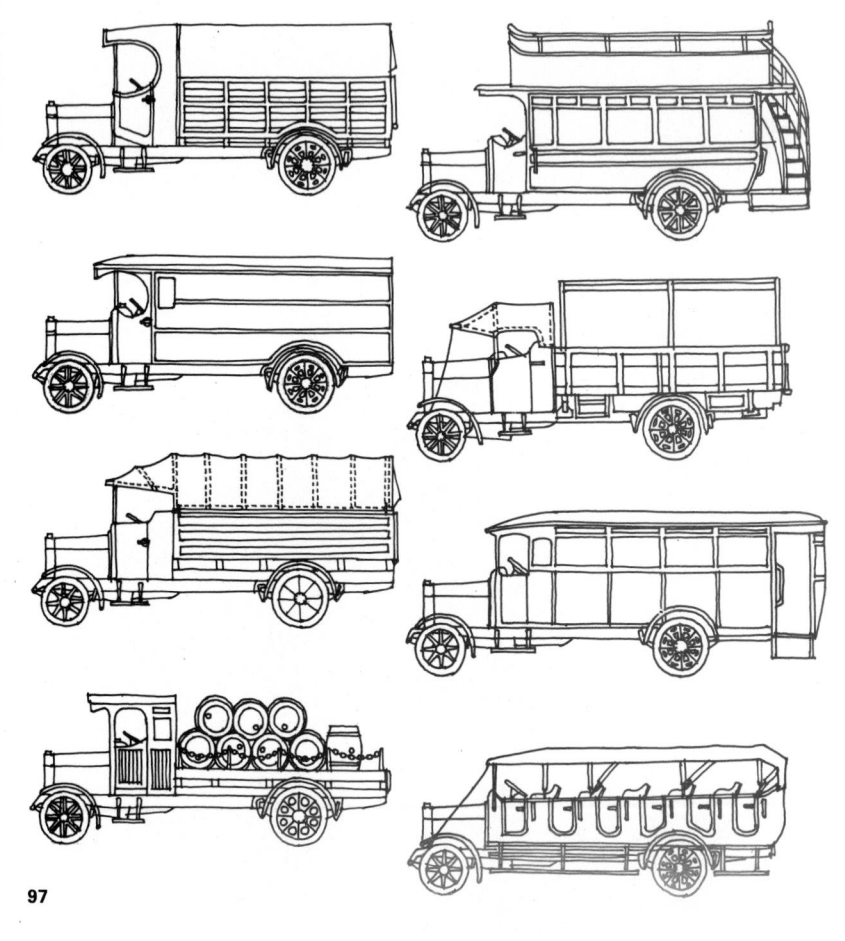

97

The versatility of the 3/5 ton chassis range is highlighted here—tank wagons, vans, lorries, buses were all built on the same chassis. Many small country businesses owned two bodies to fit one chassis, usually a charabanc for weekends and a truck for weekday work.

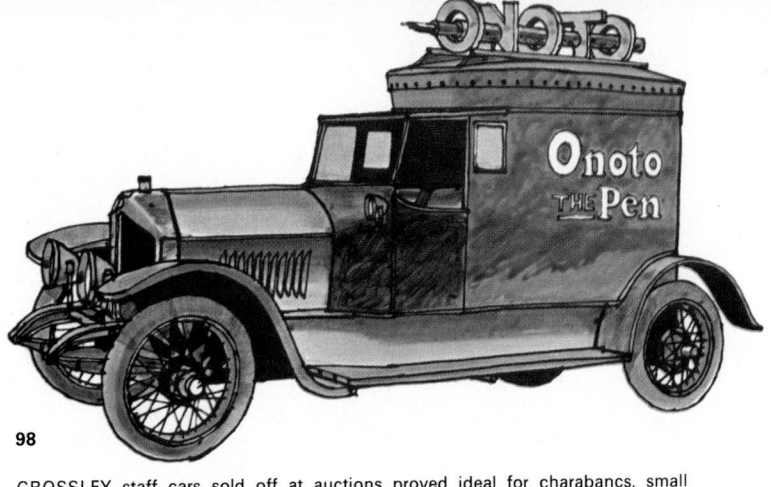

98

CROSSLEY staff cars sold off at auctions proved ideal for charabancs, small country buses, light trucks and vans. This ingenious Onoto van shows a novel way to advertise.

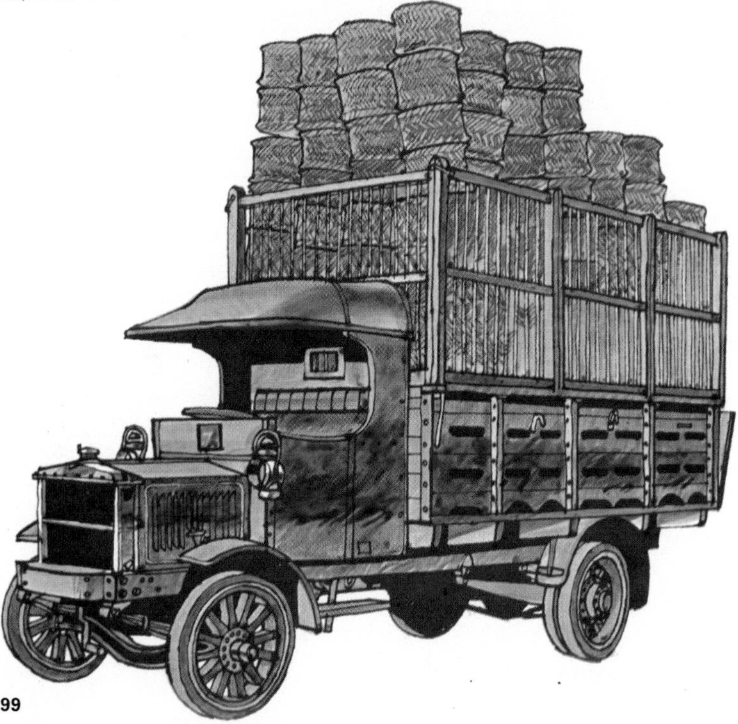

99

The British were flooded with trucks that the Americans did not want the expense of shipping home. This FEDERAL is typical of those that found a new life bringing fresh fruit to the London markets, hence saving the farmers the ruinous losses being incurred by delays on the railways.

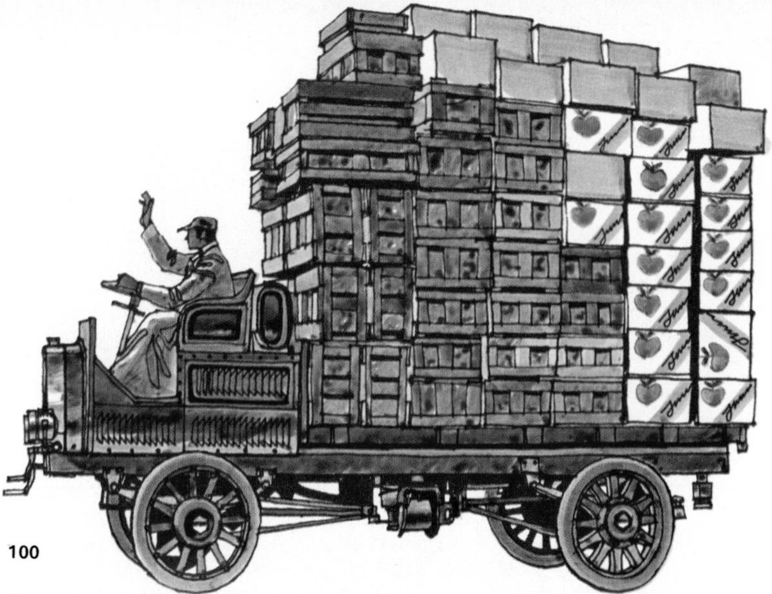

100

Many pioneers tried to perfect the four-wheel drive. The small Clintonville, Ohio, blacksmith business succeeded around 1910. The Four Wheel Drive Company had a slow start, to be saved from ruin by the Great War. The capabilities of the FWD in the swamp-like battlefields also became legend.

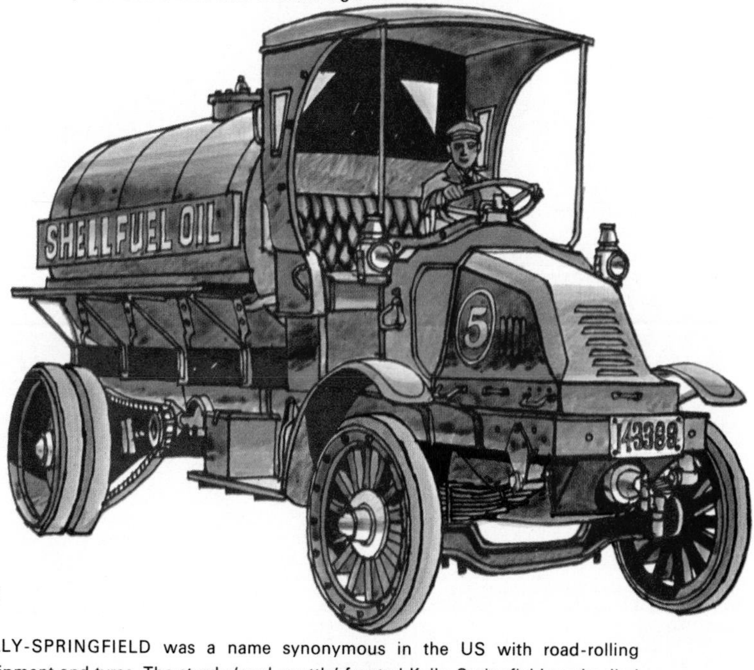

101

KELLY-SPRINGFIELD was a name synonymous in the US with road-rolling equipment and tyres. The sturdy 'coal-scuttle' fronted Kelly-Springfield trucks died away in the mid-twenties.

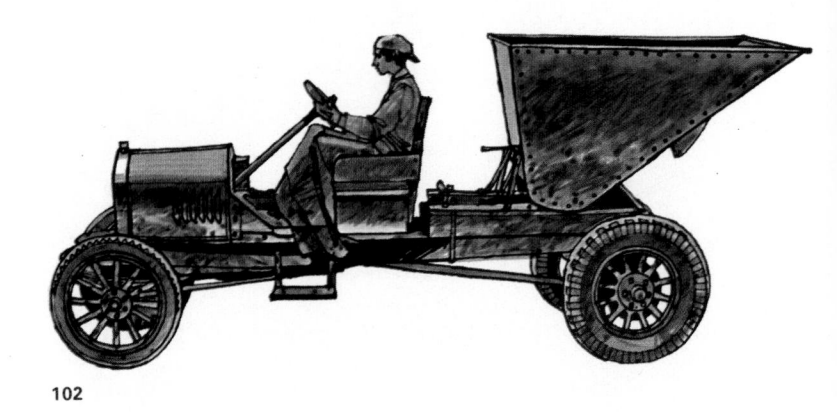

102

So popular was Henry FORD'S MODEL T car that an industry grew up offering chassis extensions and better spring for loads of 1 ton and more. Henry, seeing a market was not being satisfied, introduced his 1-ton truck version of the T in 1918.

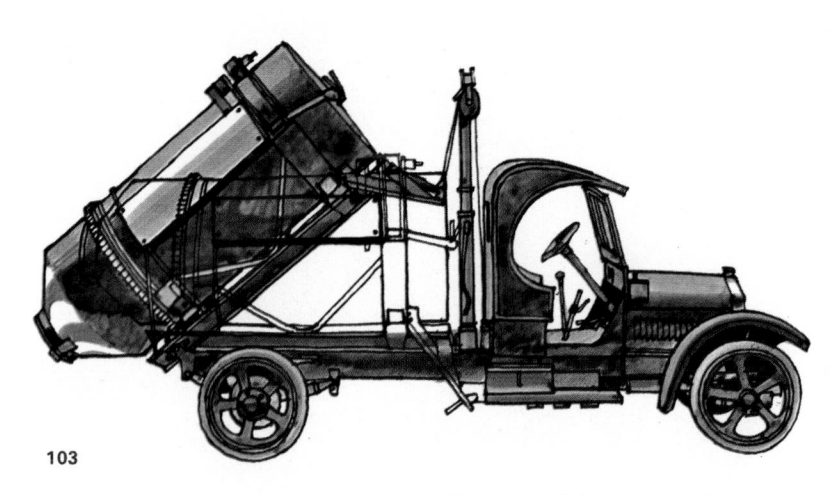

103

Building of the concrete highways in the States (forerunners of the expressways) created a new demand for the truck—concrete delivered and mixed in transit. WHITE, who supplied this chassis, were phasing out their car production in 1919 whilst Packard did the reverse.

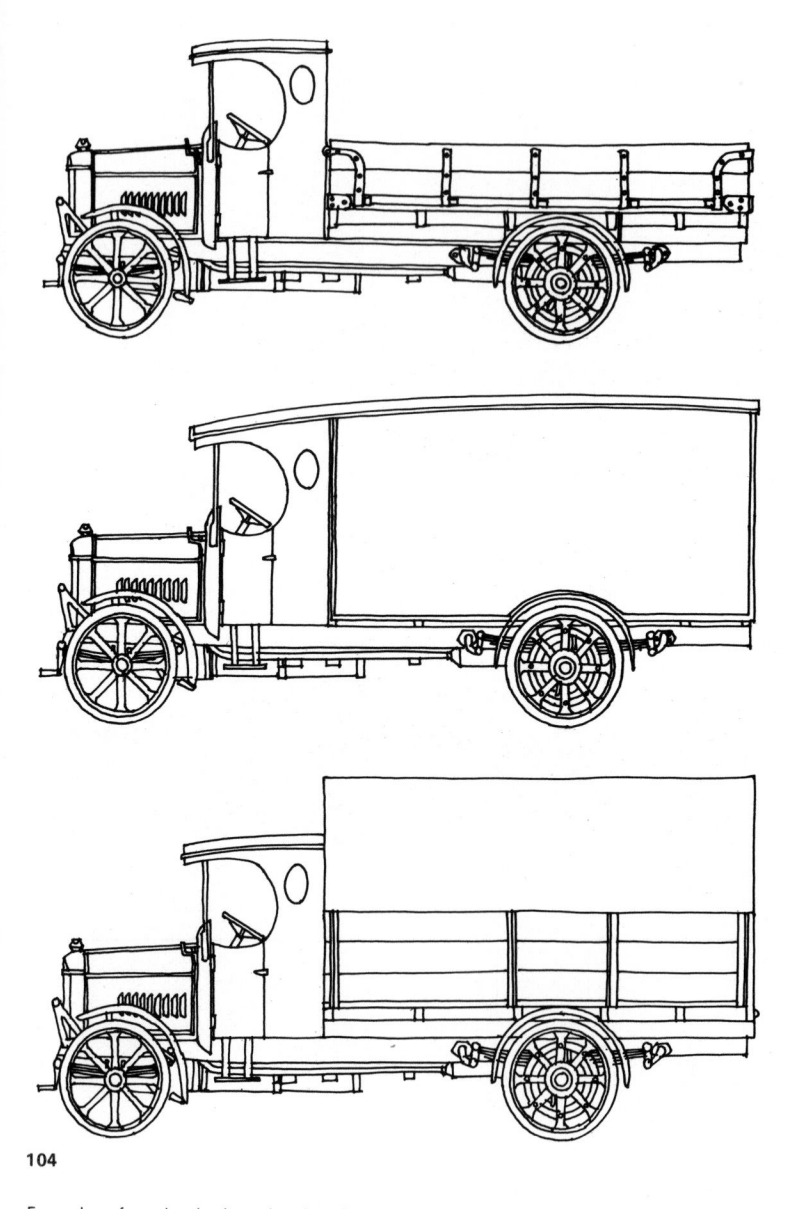

104

Examples of varying bodywork using the same cab structure on the Dennis 4-ton chassis. Dennis Brothers were pioneers of the worm axle.

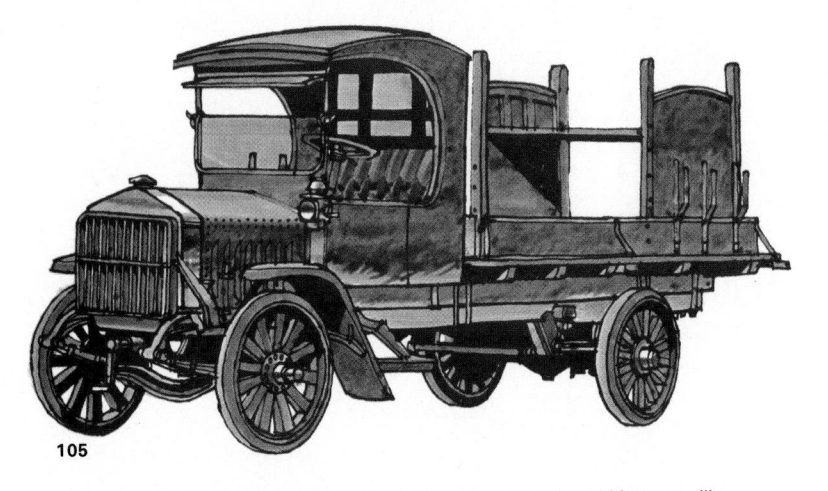

105

Although most companies had accepted the worm-drive by 1920, some, like STERLING, continued to give the customer an option.

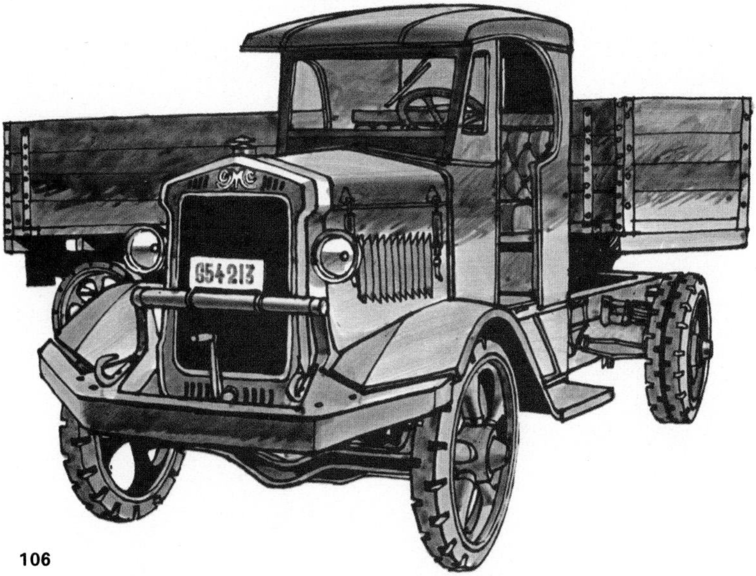

106

Six-wheelers became the vogue through the mid-twenties. GMC claimed theirs to be the first capable of 15 tons gross. The 32·4hp 4-cylinder engine drove through a 9-speed gearbox, 7 forward, 2 reverse in high or low ranges.

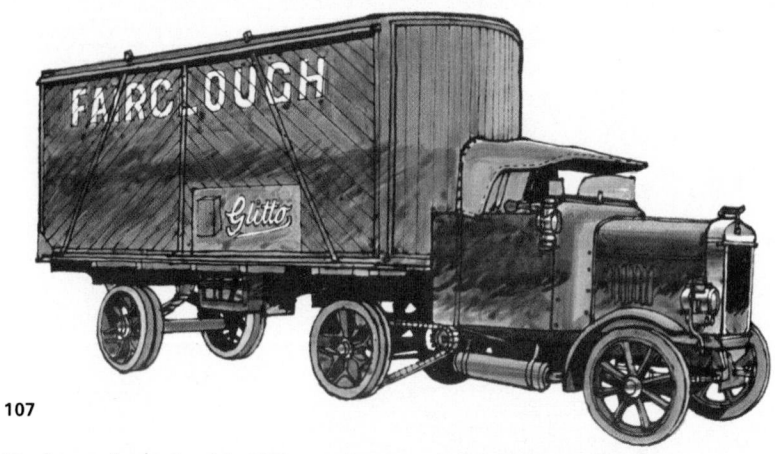

107

The Scammel, introduced in 1920, was the monarch of British roads. It was an immediate success because it offered a greater payload than other vehicles while still conforming to the laws governing the amount of weight placed on each axle.

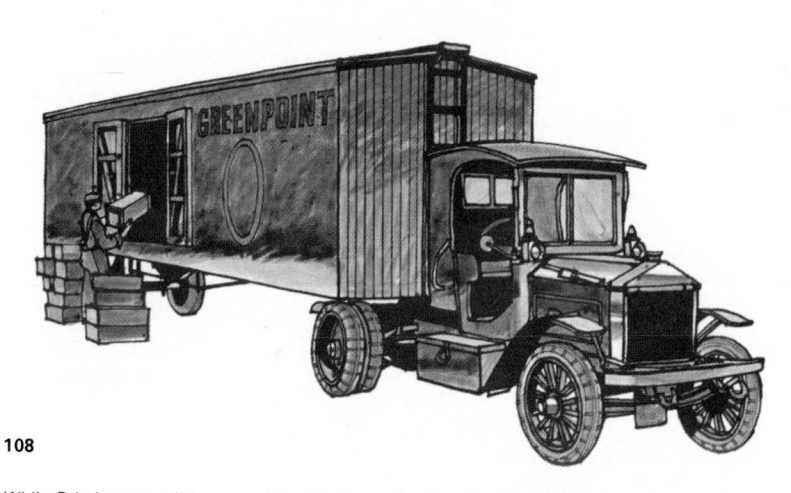

108

While Britain was still hampered by the Motor Car Act, the United States quickly came to terms with the automobile. In 1920 box trailers, 36 ft long and 8 ft wide, were to be seen on America's newly constructed concrete highways.

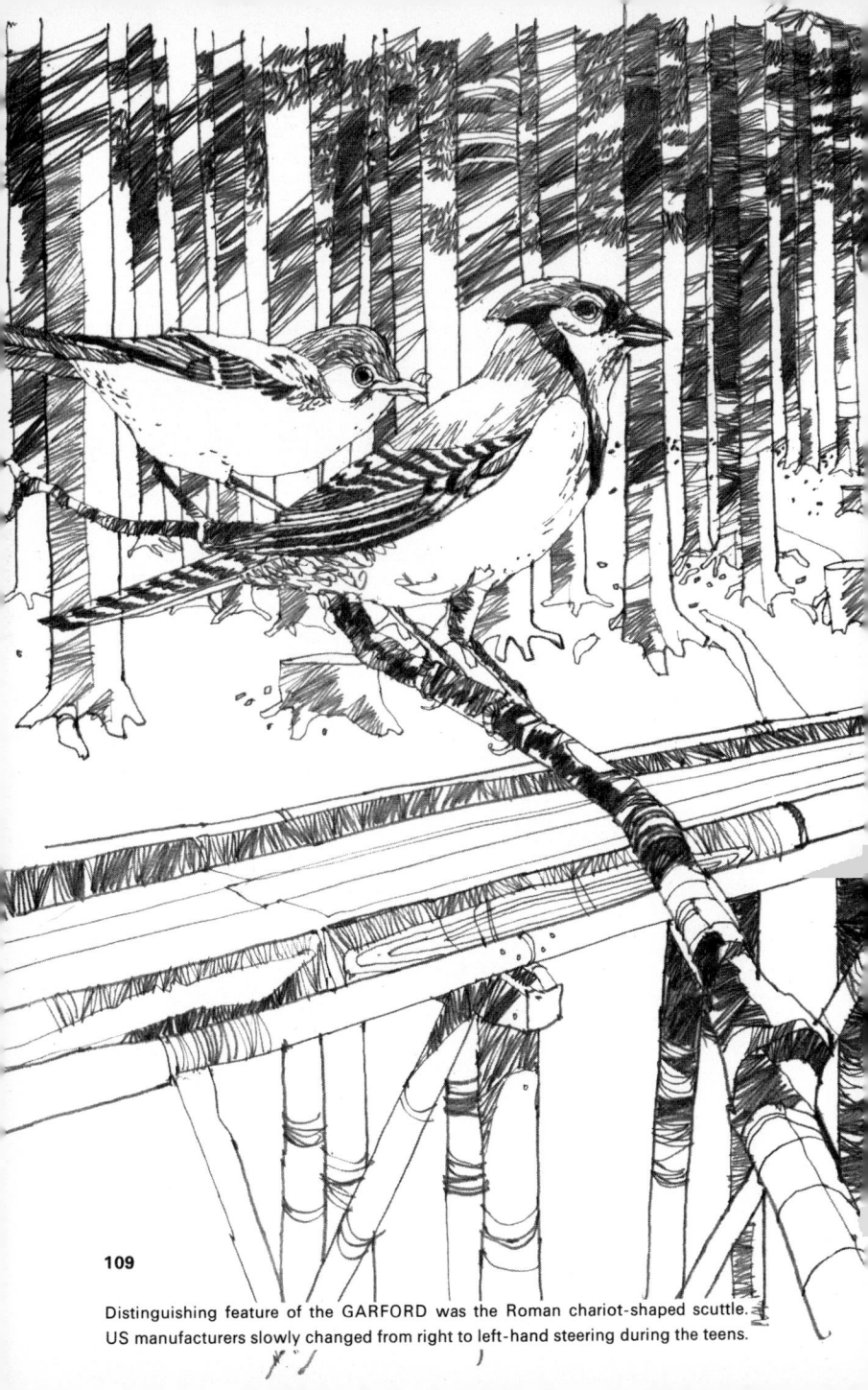

109

Distinguishing feature of the GARFORD was the Roman chariot-shaped scuttle.
US manufacturers slowly changed from right to left-hand steering during the teens.

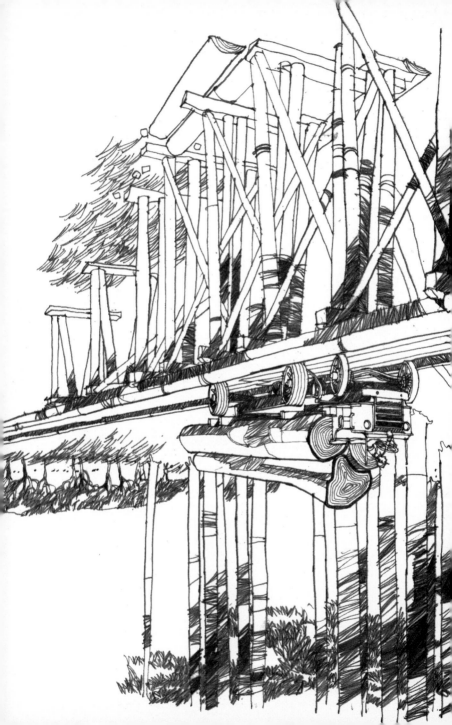

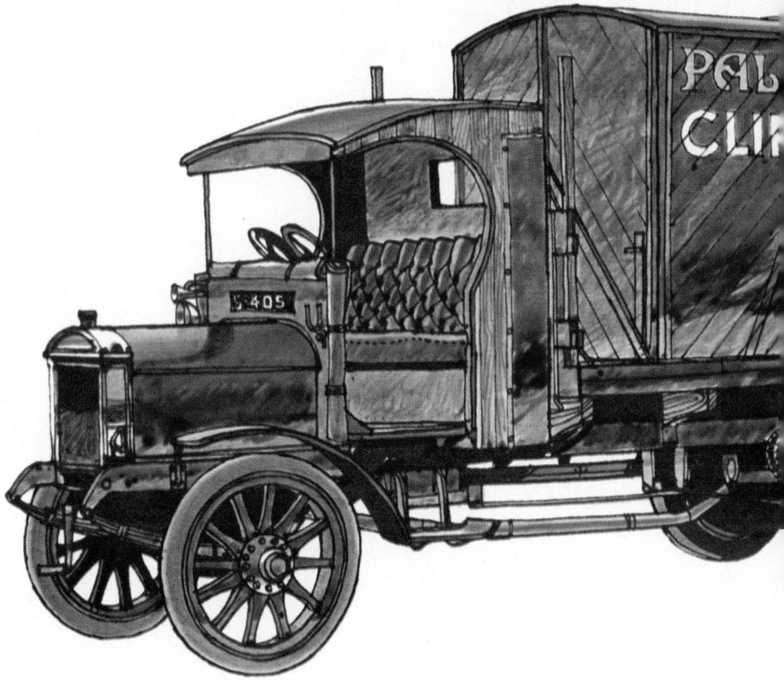

111

Drawbar trailers were prohibited in parts of Europe unless the trailer had provision
for a guard to also operate the brake.

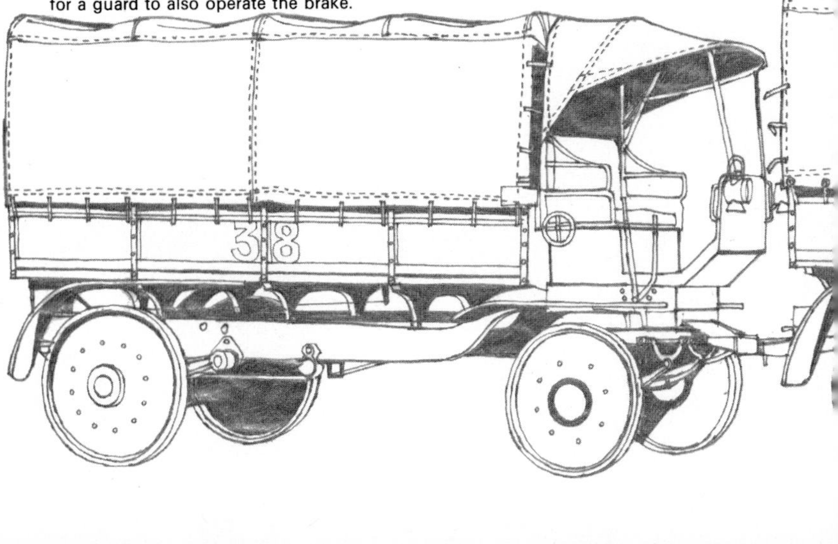

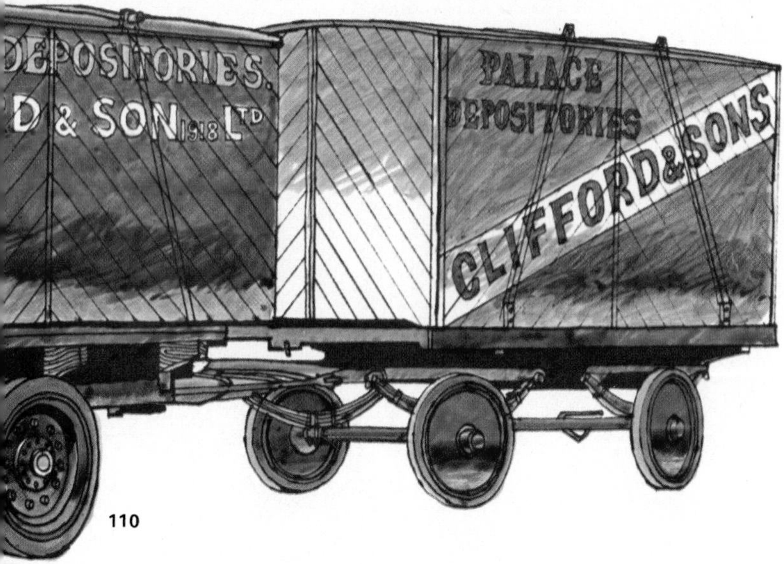

110

A 1912 Commer and draw-bar trailer, complete with lift van body, makes an impressive sight.

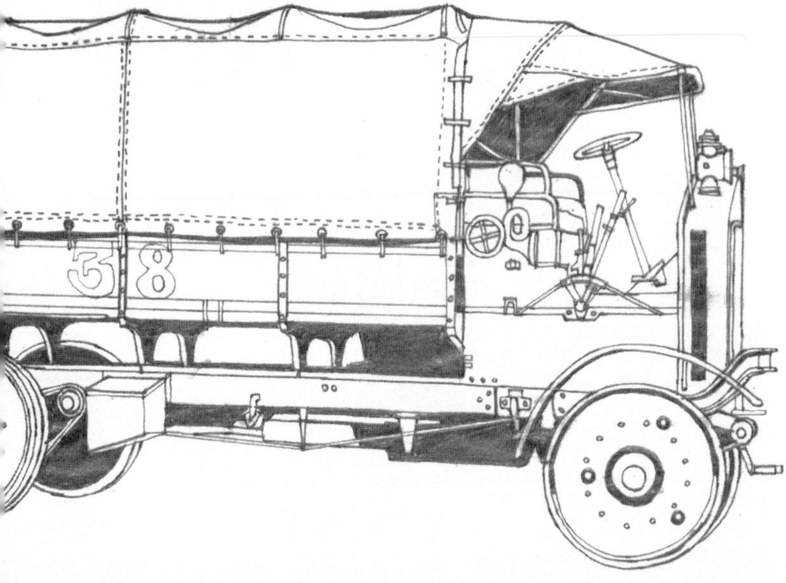

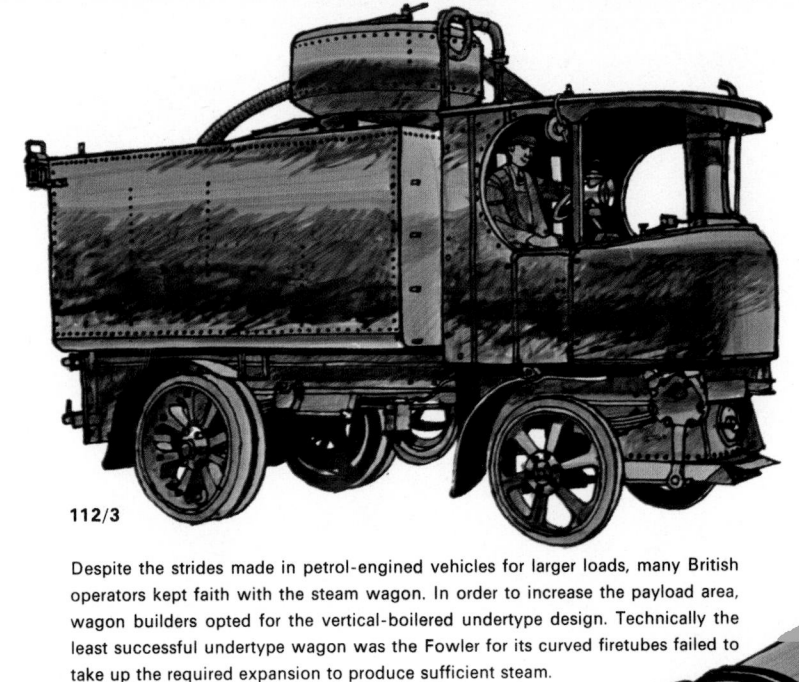

112/3

Despite the strides made in petrol-engined vehicles for larger loads, many British operators kept faith with the steam wagon. In order to increase the payload area, wagon builders opted for the vertical-boilered undertype design. Technically the least successful undertype wagon was the Fowler for its curved firetubes failed to take up the required expansion to produce sufficient steam.

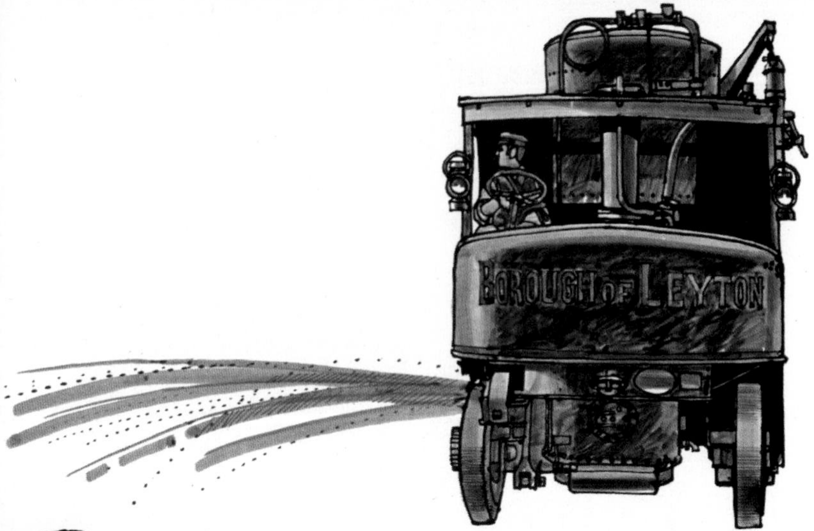

114

On the debit side, 6-wheeled artics had to contend with the deadweight for road adhesion. CHENARD WALCKER offered a tractor/trailer with their patented system that enabled the transfer of as much weight as was required to the driving wheels of the tractor.

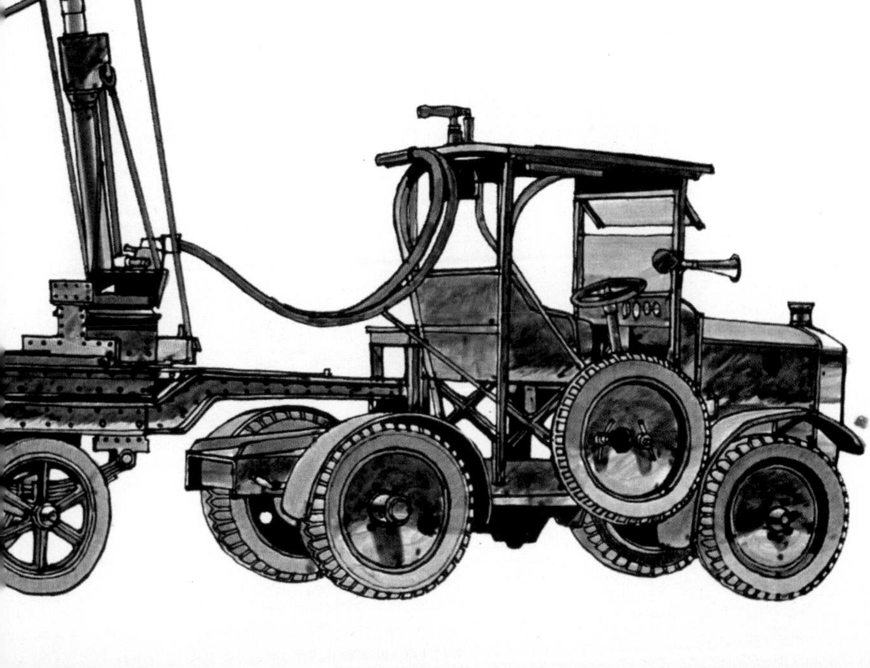

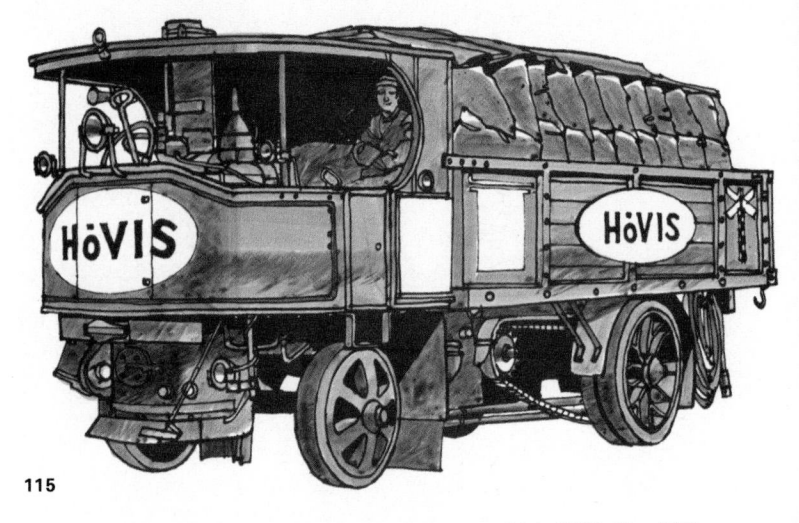

115

Garretts introduced their vertical-boilered undertype model in 1922. The CAV electric lighting is noteworthy—from 1923 lighting sets were all the rage, even on steamers.

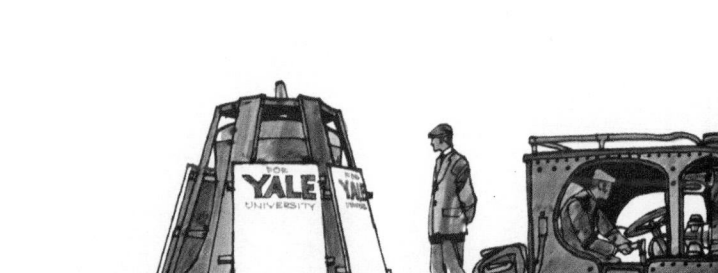

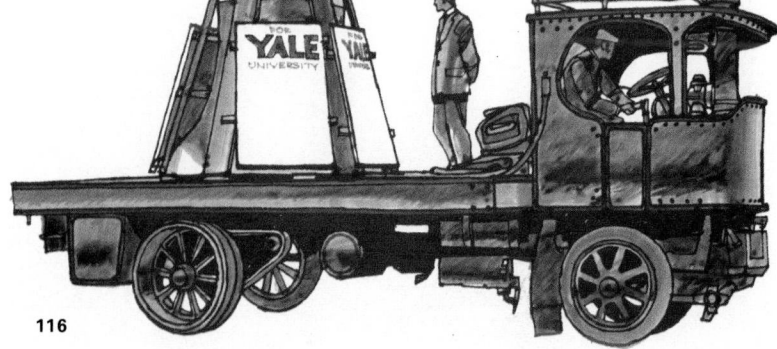

116

Stalwart of the undertype principle and in the foreground of the market was the SENTINEL.

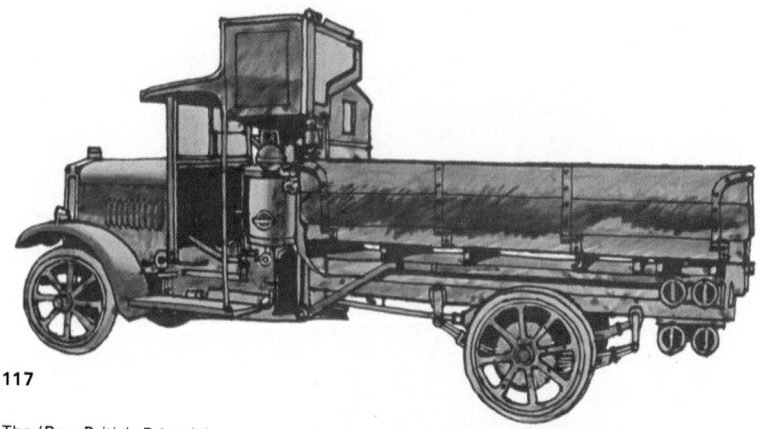

117

The 'Buy British Brigade' was never stronger than in the twenties, no doubt contributing to the continued success of steam wagons. Everything had to be home-produced where possible and as a substitute for petrol, many manufacturers, like GUY, continued to offer coal gas as an alternative.

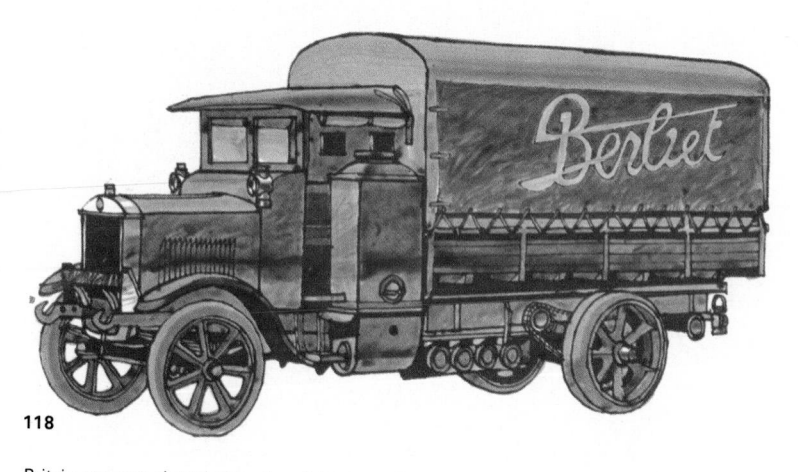

118

Britain was not alone in her chauvinist campaign as this French BERLIET shows.

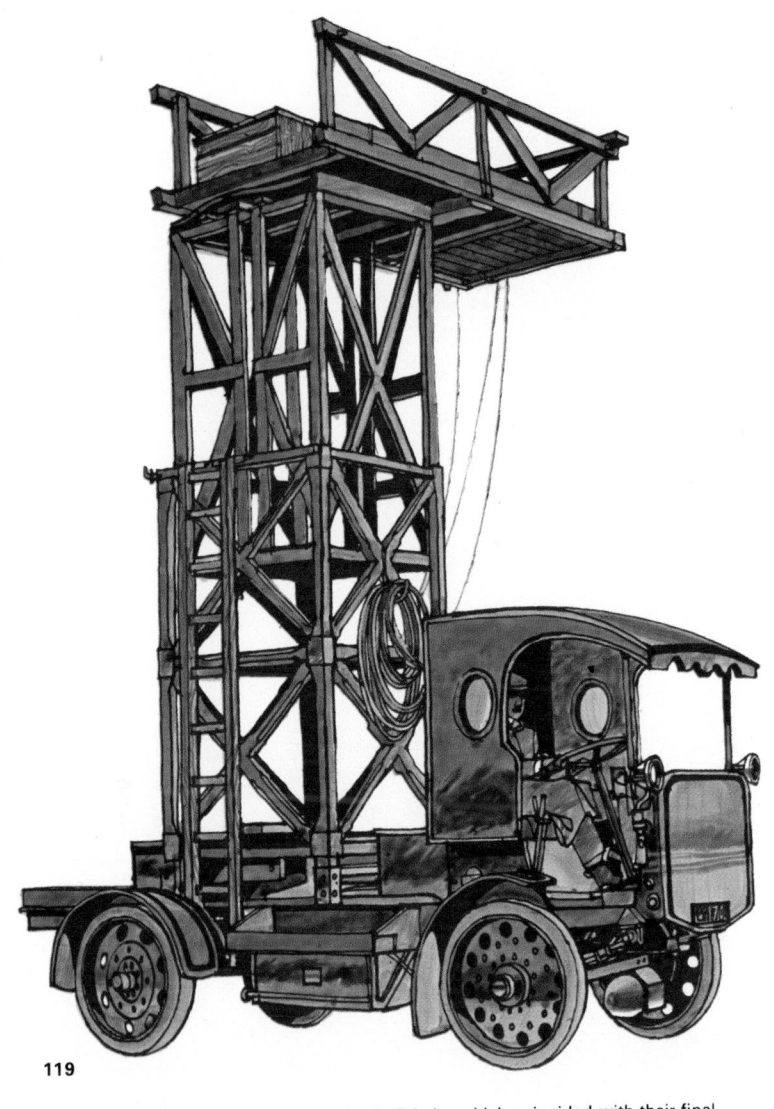

119

It also promoted an upsurge in electrics in Britain, which coincided with their final decline in the US. RANSOMES SIMS & JEFFERIES, the Suffolk steam wagon and engine builder were to the front with their Orwell electric.

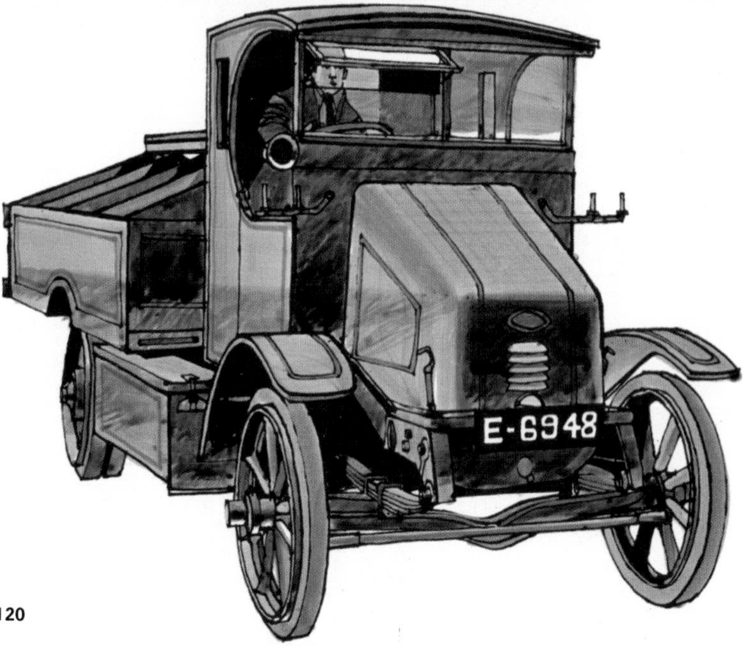

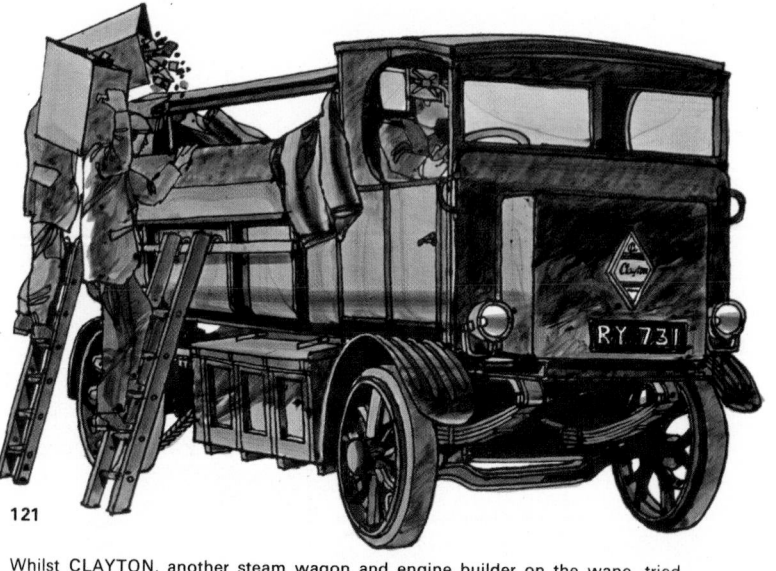

120

GUY also had a nibble at the market, but later concentrated their electric efforts towards trolleybuses.

121

Whilst CLAYTON, another steam wagon and engine builder on the wane, tried desperately hard to achieve success with a heavier range of electrics.

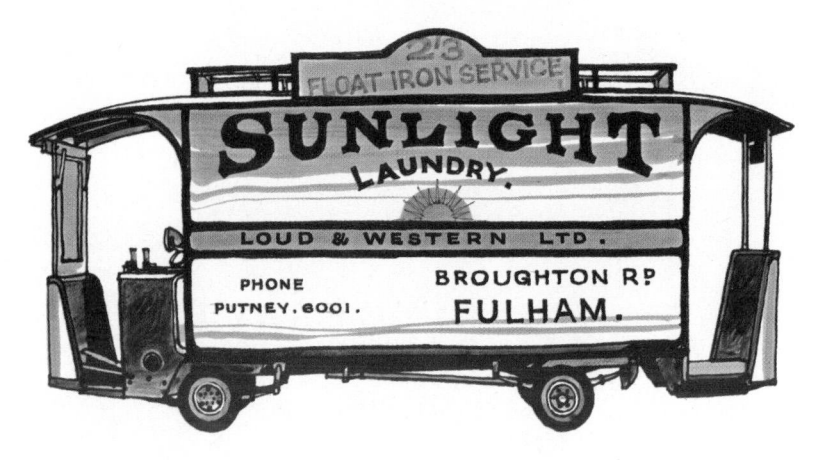

122/3

A threat to the electric truck from 1923—provided you had no conscience about the home market nonsense—was the SHELVOKE & DREWRY freighter. With a platform height of only 22 ins from the ground and a 21 ft turning circle, it was ideal for short distance and municipal deliveries. The tramlike control box meant it was also as easy to drive as an electric.

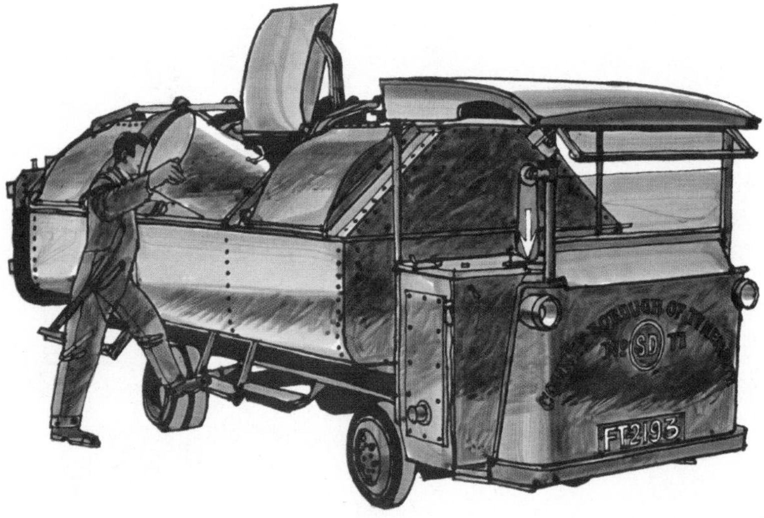

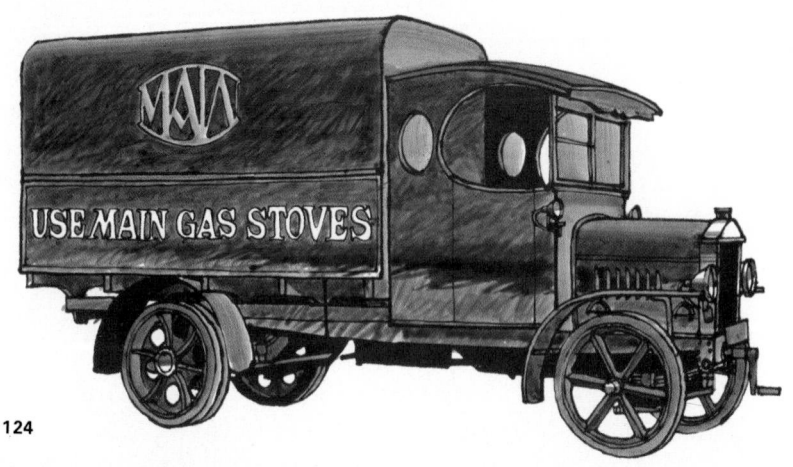

124

The AEC Company grew out of the London Motor Omnibus Co's offshoot, Motor Omnibus Construction, later absorbed by the London General Omnibus Co. Vehicles were first made only for the LMOC or LGOC needs, but the Great War brought a demand for 3- and 5-ton lorry chassis. AEC's 2-ton model, illustrated, was announced in 1922.

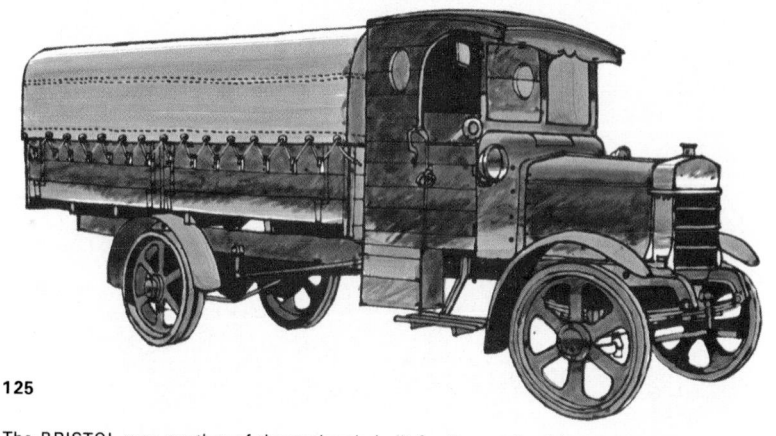

125

The BRISTOL was another of those chassis built for the needs of bus operators. When offered to the market for the first time in 1920 it offered a single-plate clutch.

126

The North Eastern Railway tried its hand at building its own vehicles long before the Great War but gave up after a year or so.

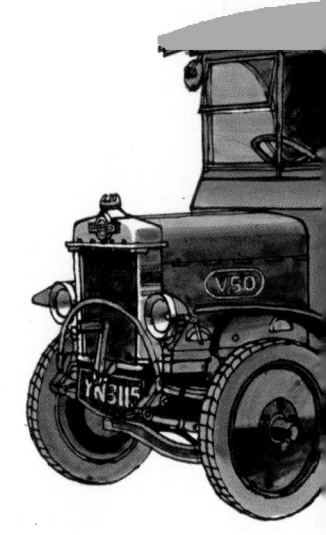

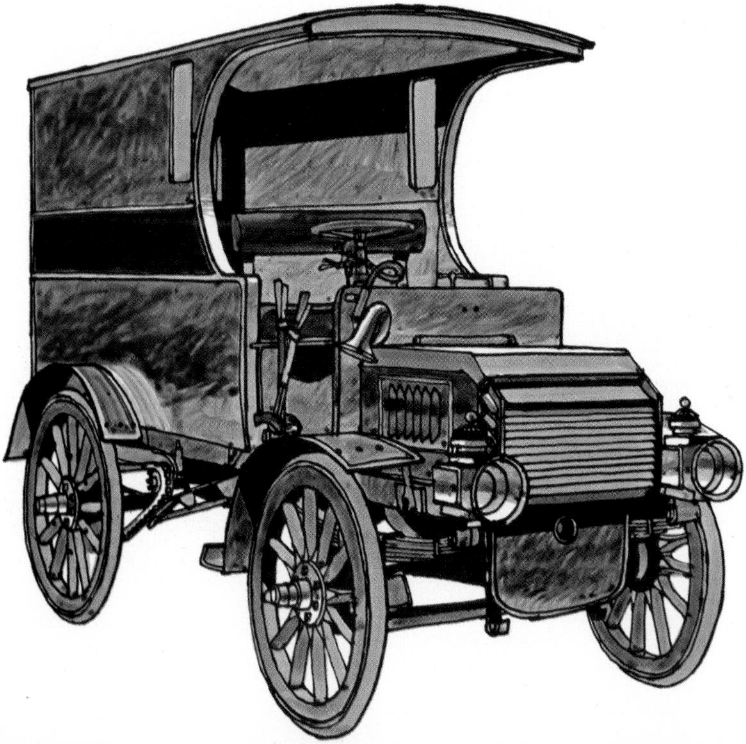

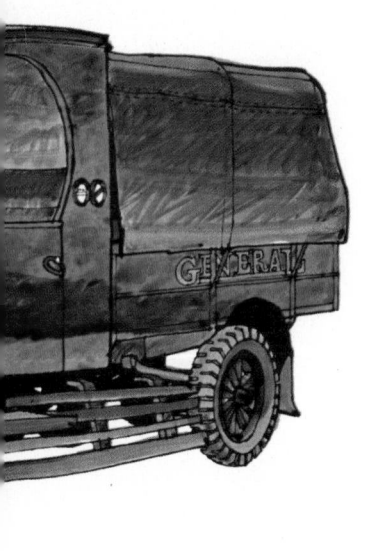

127

After successfully making its own buses, the LGOC had a second bite of the cherry in the twenties with the manufacture of $1\frac{1}{2}$ and 2 ton vans. Powered by Dorman engines, only 50 were completed and used exclusively for the company's own interdepartmental fleet.

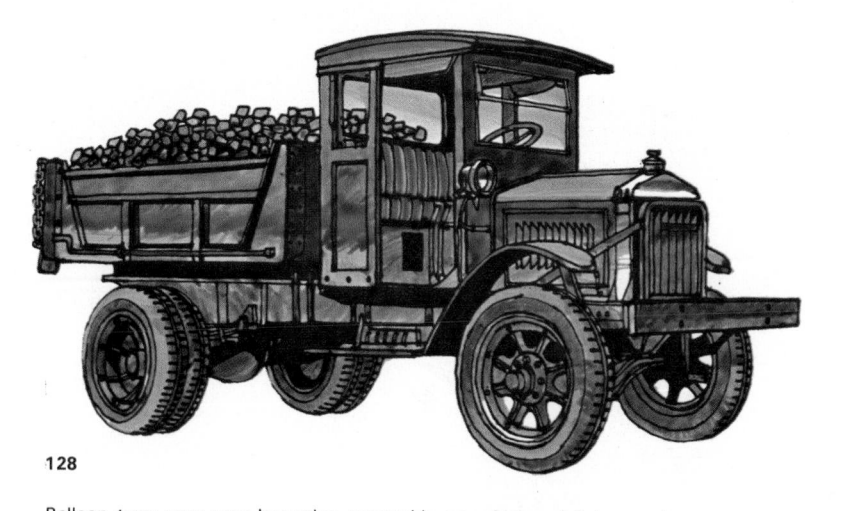

128

Balloon tyres were now becoming acceptable on vehicles of 3 tons and over. Extensive trials had taken place in the States by Goodyear. This CORBITT truck was made in Henderson, North Carolina.

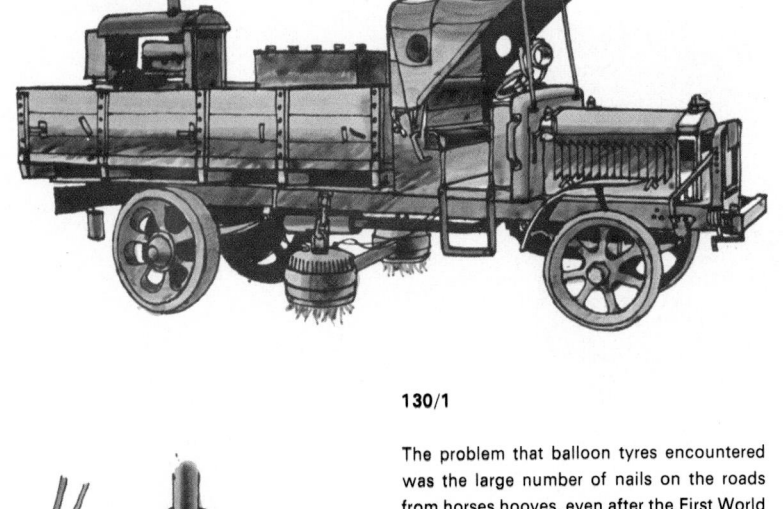

130/1

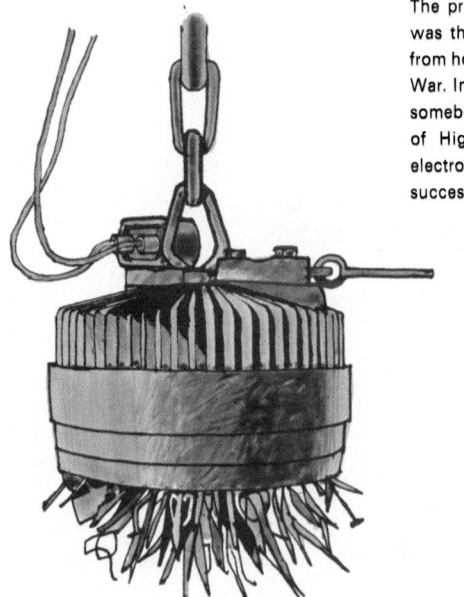

The problem that balloon tyres encountered was the large number of nails on the roads from horses hooves, even after the First World War. In an attempt to overcome the problem, somebody in the Nevada State Department of Highways dreamed up this truck with electro-magnets. Apparently it had some success. Did the idea spread to other cities?

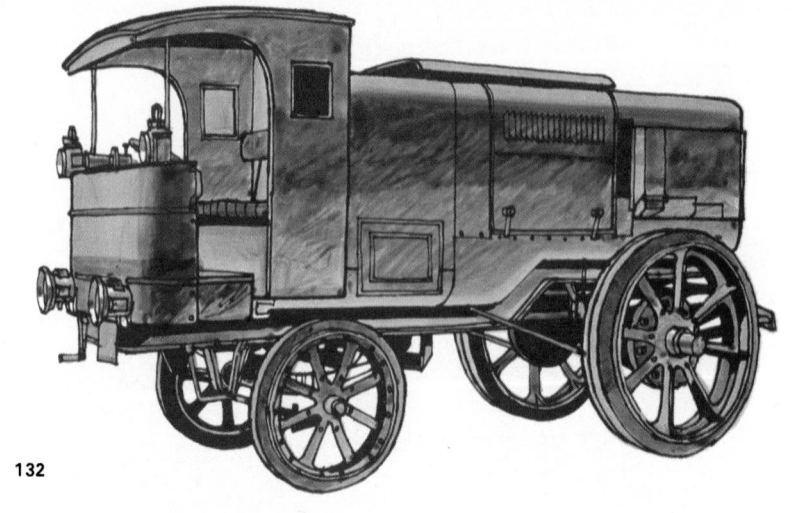

132

Road-railers were another talked-of feature of the twenties. GUY offered this tractor in 1923 but sold practically none.

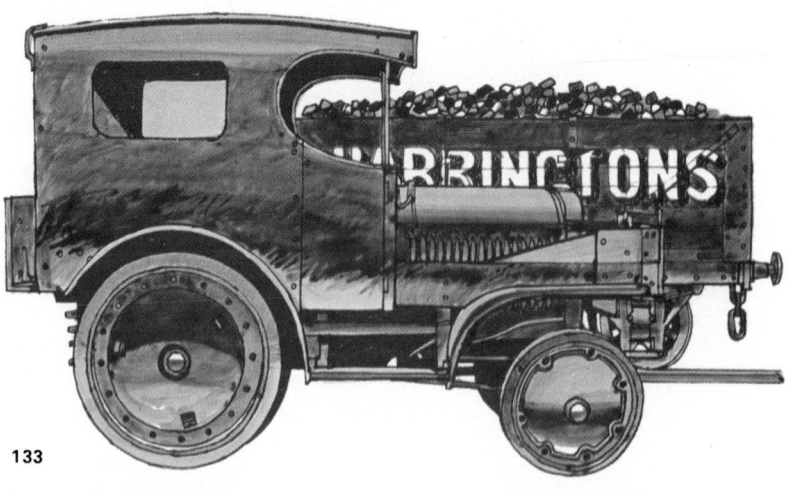

133

A much more versatile and successful heavy-duty tractor was the McCORMICK-DEERING, known later as the INTERNATIONAL. Capable of handling 30 tons, it became a common sight in railway yards, on the farm, or hauling trailers, and even as a one-man crane.

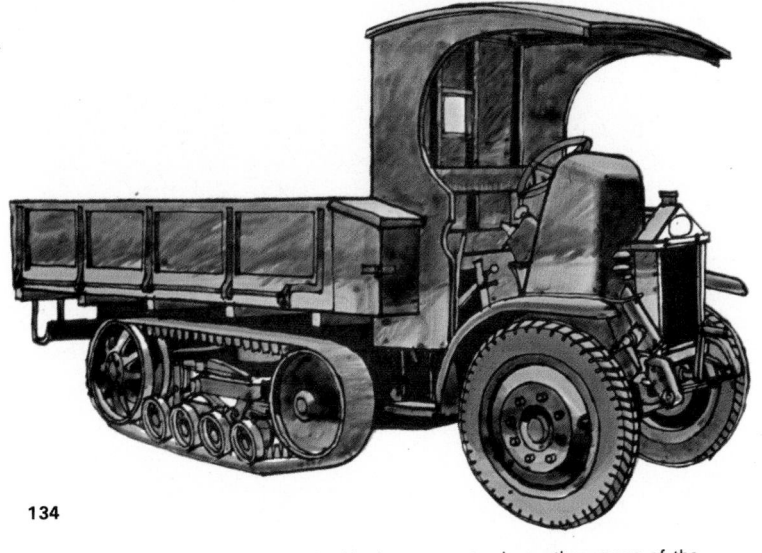

134

Kegresse was the name associated with the creeper track, another vogue of the twenties. The fusion of the talents of Monsieur Kegresse and H. G. Burford Ltd produced the BURFORD-KEGRESSE. The creeper track enabled vehicles to travel over the roughest ground, snow and desert.

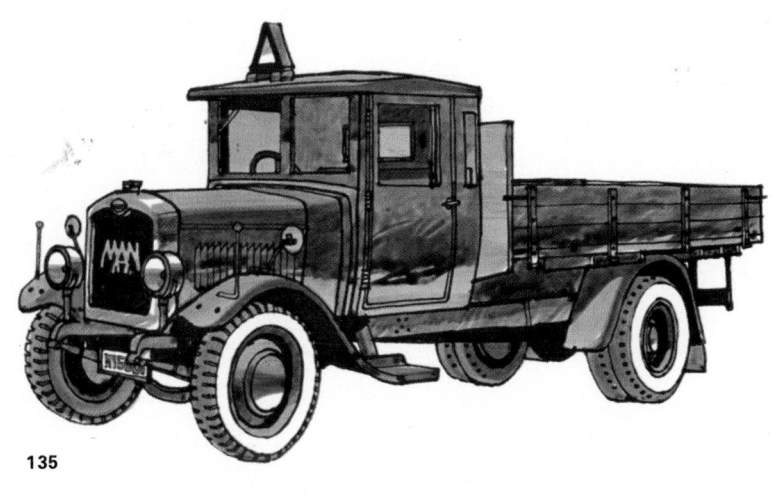

135

And the oil engine was another idea, although often dismissed. MAN stole the lead in 1924 by announcing the world's first practicable oil engine for a truck at the Berlin Motor Show. The refined lines of this 1926 MAN suggest a vehicle some 5 or 6 years newer.

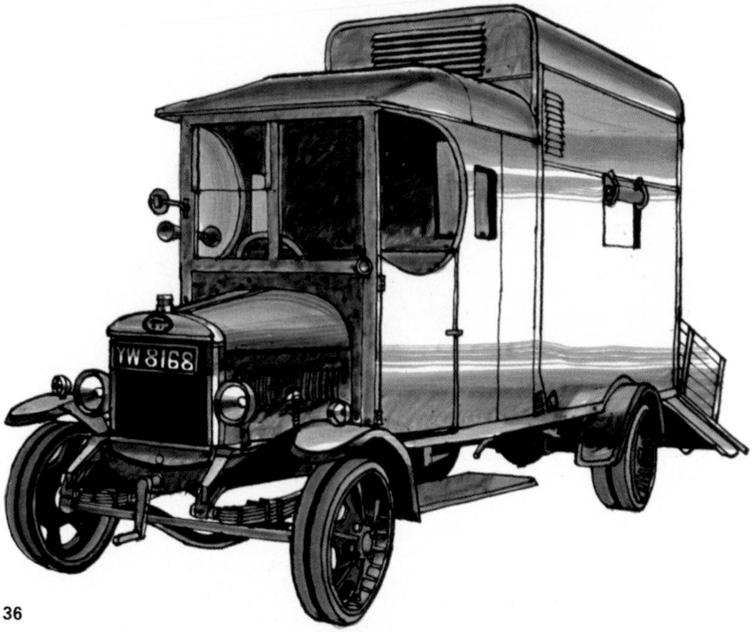

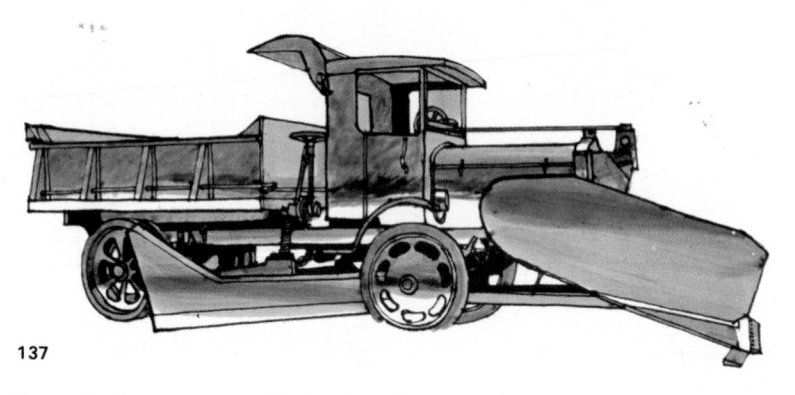

136

The carriage of racehorses is a very specialised business and Vincents of Reading have been providing boxes for this need for many years. This box, designed for 2 horses, with a place for a vet, is on a GUY chassis.

137

Snow ploughs are more municipal gadgets. The 4-wheel drive WALTER snow plough was a common sight in the United States and still is. Walter specialise in 4-wheel drive, fire appliances, snow ploughs and cross-country vehicles.

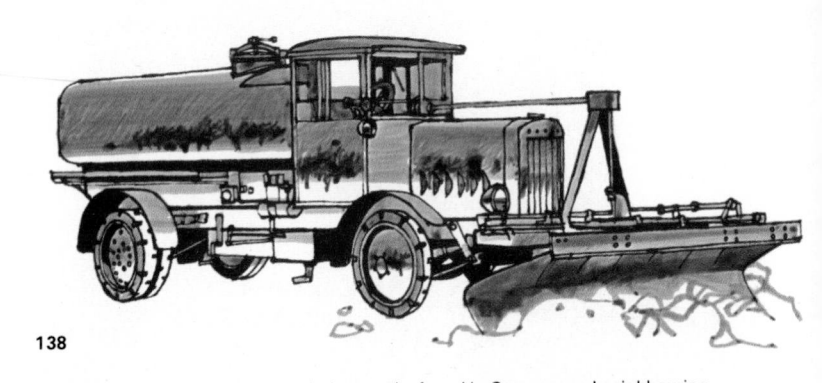

138

And the BUSSING of a similar period was to be found in Germany and neighbouring countries.

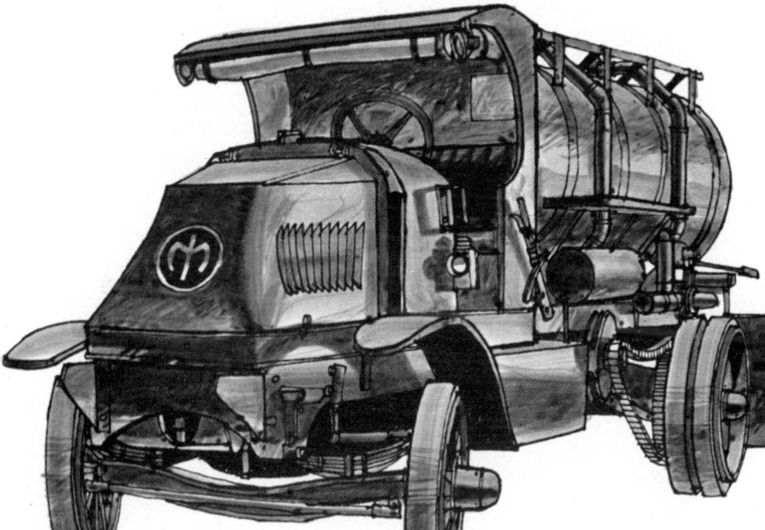

139

When the MACK name reappeared in 1914 with the introduction of the AC Model, it was to immortalise MACK forever. For its sturdiness, the soldiers called it the Bulldog and then came the legend 'built like a Mack'.

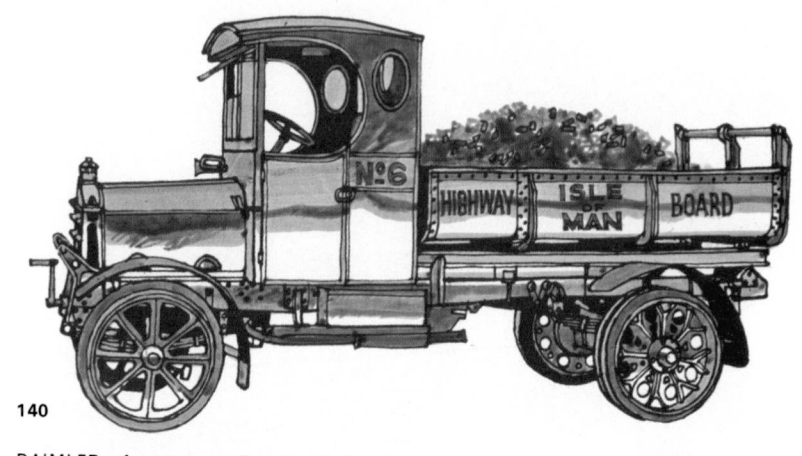

140

DAIMLER, of course, persevered with their famous sleeve-valve engine, even in their bus and truck range.

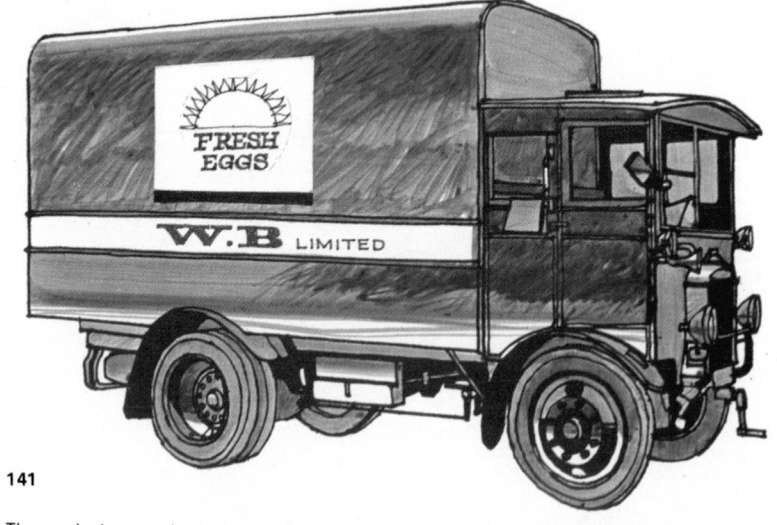

141

The marketing amalgamation of Daimler and AEC produced a shortlived new name on British roads—the ASSOCIATED DAIMLER commonly referred to as ADC. It was offered with either the AEC or Daimler sleeve valve engine.

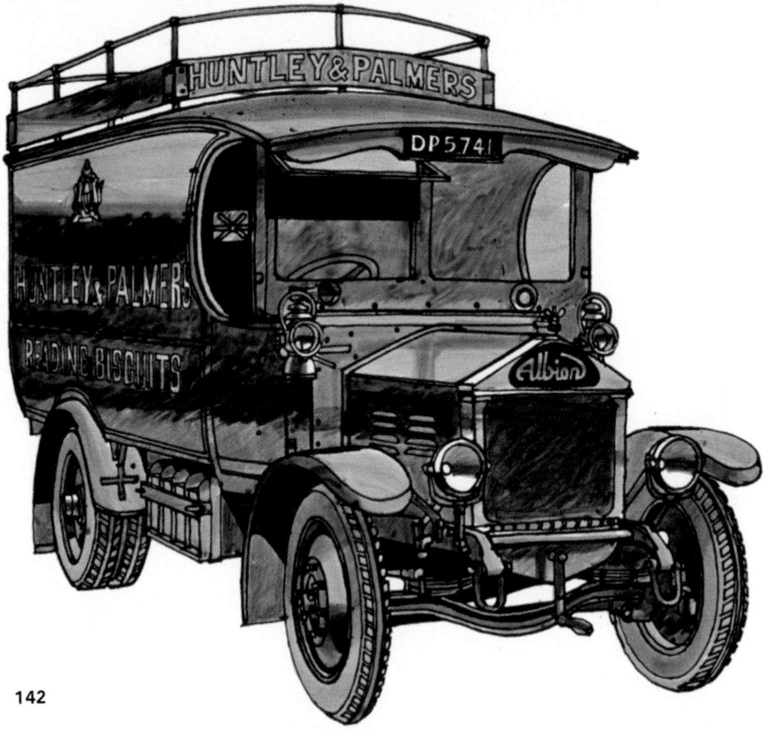

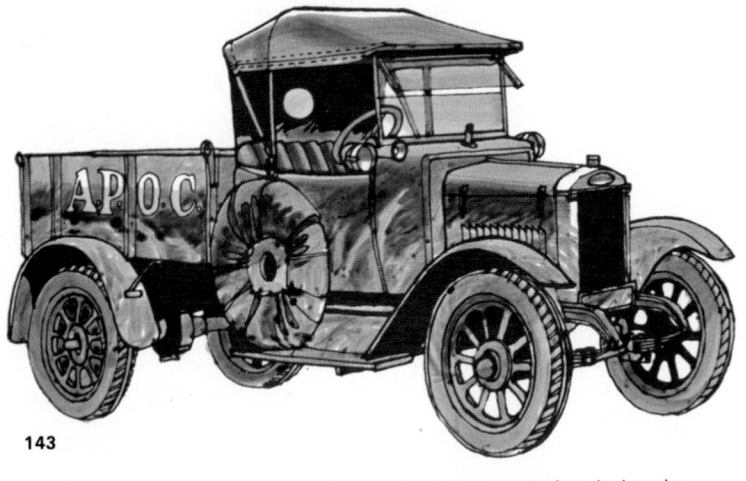

142

The average British 2-ton van of the twenties is typified by this ALBION. Note the nice curved side windows for the driver—a hangover from the horse van days.

143

The British had very little to offer in the way of a 1-ton range before the introduction of the MORRIS in 1924. Until then, car chassis were utilised or the buyer had to look to the foreign market.

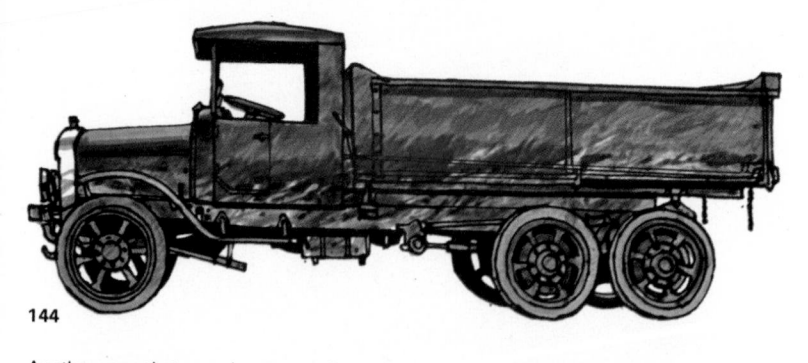

144

Another craze that was about to catch on was the rigid 6-wheeler. Several experiments had taken place in France, Britain and the US, but one of the first to be commercially marketed was the Californian-built MORELAND, offered with either a 4- or 6-cylinder engine.

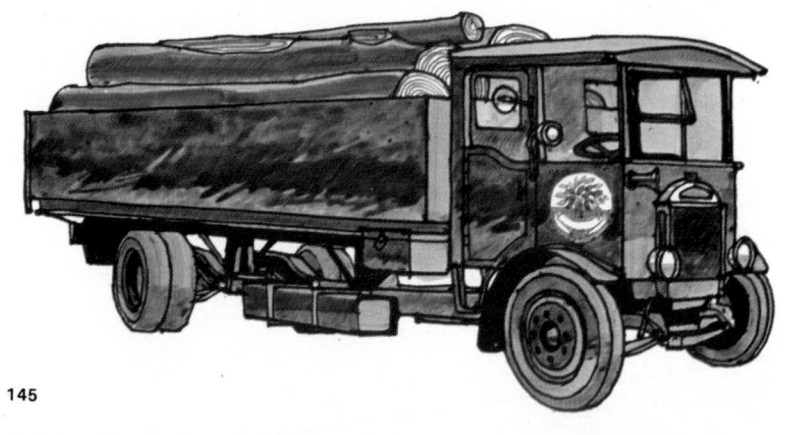

145

Until the mid-twenties buses had been built on lorry chassis with modifications like higher gear ratio axles and better springing, but now the demand was increasing for buses to have their own chassis to suit their specialised needs. The trend was for L-head in-line 6-cylinder engines and dropped chassis frames. Thus, buses tended to become the best private car chassis and, as the late Sir Laurence Pomeroy would have us believe, certain car chassis became more like lorries. Some truck manufacturers also thought that the new bus qualities could be offered for some commercial haulage users. MAUDSLAY was one of the first in Britain. Note also the new vogue this side of the Atlantic—cab-over-the-engine. Garford and Autocar, the last two exponents of this US principle, were finally about to abandon it.

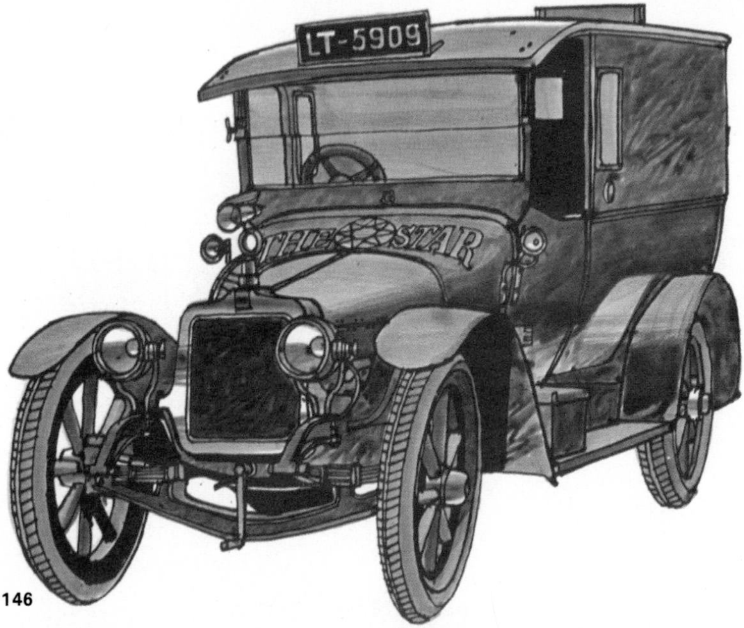

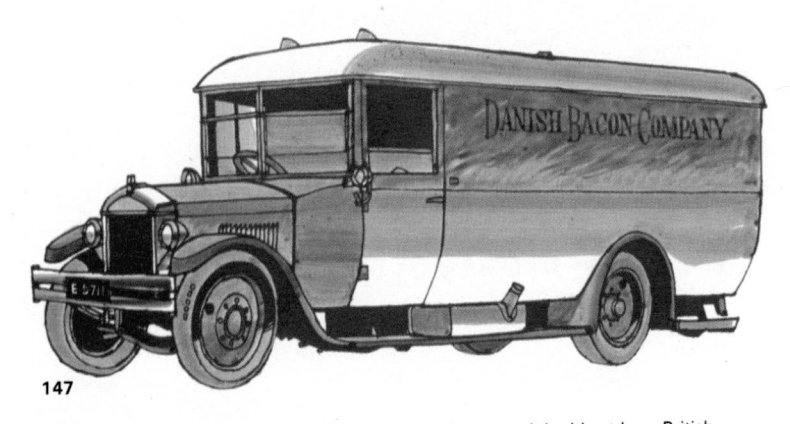

146

Newspaper proprietors needing speed often chose car chassis such as CLEMENT-TALBOT, and had bodies built to their requirements. Balloon tyres for light vans, trucks and cars had been used since Edwardian days.

147

The new drop frame 6-cylinder 'low-line' for 1927 was exploited best by a British newcomer, GILFORD. The chassis were made up of component parts employing such American products as Buda and Lycoming engines and Timkin axles.

THE HARD WAY AND THE EASY WAY

Engineering design is a – perhaps *the* – liberal art. It is Art in that every designer has his own way of solving the problems, and every way is 'right' in that the parts fit together, the truck does roll – if not, we would not call him an engineer. But there is a way of finding out which of all the different designs is best, they can compete, and everyone must agree that the one which wins is the best one; a field in which agreement can be reached deserves to be called liberal.

The first thirty or fifty years of the history of the truck is a story of the competition between two main approaches, the easy way and the hard way. The easy way to make a truck is to separate out all the different functions and do them in separate components. One has a furnace, into which go fuel and air and out of which comes high-temperature, low-pressure gas. One has a steam generator, into which goes high-temperature gas and out of which comes high-pressure vapour. One has an expander, into which goes high-pressure vapour and out of which comes mechanical work. The steam engine is a classic example of the easy way to build an engine; because all the stages of turning chemical energy into mechanical work are separated, one can be stopped without stopping the others, the steam engine can start itself and its load from a standstill.

And steam engines were not only easy to understand, they were easy to build and to repair. The boilers were assembled by closing rivets, one after another, and expanding tubes, one after another. The piston rods had glands that were packed by hand and tightened down periodically. The connecting rod bearings were loaded with a wedge so that wear could occur – and wear *must* occur if an engine starts from rest under load – and the bearing clearance be restored.

The steam truck was similarly simple throughout. Steering was by a worm and wheel, and completely irreversible. The suspension did allow all of the wheels to share the load, but had a forbidding resemblance to that of a railway wagon. Most notably, tyres were solid, steel at first and only later hard rubber.

But very early there appeared radicals, designers who chose to do things the hard way, to build trucks with internal combustion engines that were not comprehended even by the designers. (The mechanics of the piston ring sliding on a film of oil were clarified only in the last five years or so, and in the case of the diesel engine the theory of the combustion process is still a happy hunting ground for university research departments.) The internal combustion engine turns chemical energy to work in one stroke, or at most four, and it sets out to contain pressures and temperatures that, if sustained, would destroy iron or aluminium. The internal combustion engine is essentially a high-speed engine, and it is not easy to build nor to repair; if a bearing fails, it is immediately wiped out and all the operator can do is stop the engine before any further damage is done.

The internal combustion engine cannot start itself from rest and has only a narrow-speed range, so that it needs a gearbox with different ratios which can be shifted while on the move – again, a hard way to go.

And the radical designers adopted the pneumatic tyre, another device whose theory is baffling – only ten years ago did Eric Gough at Fort Dunlop point out how a tyre which is itself everywhere in tension can serve the purpose of keeping wheel and road apart; the wheel hangs in the bead wires. The tyre, like the internal combustion engine, poses daunting problems to manufacture and to repair.

But by 1927 it was clear beyond cavil that the radicals were right, that the hard way was the way to go. Steam trucks had abandoned simplicity, and gone to flash boilers which needed the fuel feed and the water feed to be controlled simultaneously with the power output, the steamers had suspension and steering and tyres like those of motor trucks.

There was no element of chance or luck in this outcome; given free competition, the radicals had to win. The solid tyre was cheap and, at low speeds, reliable, but it demanded a strong road – ideally, of course, a steel rail! The pneumatic tyre was expensive and troublesome, but it could go over cheaply-constructed highways. And the investment in the tyre could be written off quickly, because the tyre was used for hours each day, whereas the highway was actually loaded only one-hundredth or one-thousandth of the time and had to last and last and last. . . . Thus improvements in tyres came into service quickly. Similarly, the internal combustion engine was expensive – but the expense was incurred in the

factory, for tools that could do fine work fast, and those tools were worked hard and scrapped quickly and replaced by improved tools. Once engines were being built in quantity, the cost went down and the quality went up.

In free competition, improvement is the name of the game; it is the nature of intelligent life that by the time it has built one tyre, or one truck, or one tool, it has thought of a better way to build tyres, or trucks, or tools. This is the advantage of the motor truck over the steam truck, as it is the advantage of the truck over the railway; it can be used and discarded and replaced by something better *quickly,* it exploits the power of the intellect to change, to learn, to progress. The radical approach, the hard way, won out because there was on its side the invisible hand – intelligence.

In recent years, even more ambitious engines, particularly highly rated two-strokes and turbo-charged diesel engines, have forced their way to prominence. However, this has not happened as a result of free competition: designers have been trapped between maximum weight limits and taxes on fuel heavier by far than needed to pay for the highways.

Today the lessons of early history are clear and easy to see. We see also that the same trends are continuing; vehicles of very high performance, with low-pressure tyres and even with air cushions to reduce the ground pressure, are being built to operate over the most primitive of cleared tracks. But it is still the case that the secret of success is to make the most use of human intellect, to gamble on learning taking place. And it is not only back at the factory or at the repair shop that this holds good. The radical designers took away from the driver the need to stoke the engine with fuel. They eliminated the need to keep the feed water level up. They very quickly put an end to the driver having to work the steering through several turns and then drive it back again. They spent money and ingenuity to save the driver having to use his muscles and to avoid his having to do boring, tedious control tasks fit only for a machine. But never did the designers lend a thought to save the driver from using his head, to restrict his choice of what course to steer, what ratio to engage, what speed to run at. The exceptions which could be cited only prove the rule. Power-operated gearshifts there are, automatic gearshifts there are few, because the man looking through the windshield can always make better decisions than a black box – and the exception is on public service vehicles which are driven by numerous different individuals, so that one particular driver does not learn whether

he is achieving good or bad fuel utilisation. And the tougher competition becomes, the more reliance must be placed on the human element; even a big, efficient firm, able to buy fleets of trucks at discount rates, finds that costs can be cut by letting every driver own his own truck and paying him a price at which he is glad to haul the firm's trailers.

COMMER – COMMERCIAL CARS LTD

One of the finest early makes of truck was the Commer, made by Commercial Cars of Luton – the name 'Commer' being an obvious abbreviation of 'Commercial'. Among the many people and firms who thought Commer was the best was the well-established retailer of high-class motorcars, Wyckoff Church & Partridge, New York. They boldly stated that after two years of exhaustive efficiency and economy tests, conducted by experts in the US and abroad, the Commer was the world's most efficient and economical high duty motor truck. Six miles on one gallon of fuel was quite an achievement in those days for a 3-ton lorry. Its other great asset was the Linley constant mesh gearbox with steering column change; the word pre-selective was not used in those days.

Before the First World War constant mesh, usually referred to the Lanchester or planetary gearbox principle, claimed to be superior because it avoided drivers 'crunching the gears', and gear changing was a prime difficulty encountered by many drivers, particularly those accustomed to the horse. Missing a gear had its dangers, too, particularly on a hill, where if it was missed nothing held the truck other than the brake. Of course, there were a good many who liked the sliding gear (Panhard system) for exactly the possibility of coasting downhill and generally saving fuel.

City to city endurance runs presaged a vogue for coast-to-coast feats. And feats they all were. Highways up until the late teens did not exist beyond the city limits in the States. Streets led through open fields, eventually becoming nothing more than stagecoach trails, uneven and full of potholes. In the summer the earth would dry into dust inches deep, while the reverse occurred in the winter and spring months. Then vehicles had to trundle through deep mud, making little progress for days. Bridges were also frail and often collapsed under the weight of a car, let alone a truck. So when Wyckoff Church & Partridge arranged for one of Wana-maker's store's Commers to take a 4-ton load, plus six men, from New York to Philadelphia (a distance of $119\frac{1}{2}$ miles) and back, it was considered a great event. The truck left New York at 3.33 am

...80 am the same morning. The
...inutes. Allowing 35
...favour-
...ng with
almo...

A much gre... ...r of 1911
when the Chicago Mo... ...to carry its
baggage from Chicago to Ind... ...returned to
New York via Indiana, Michigan, Ohio, ...ania and New
York states, covering 2,535 miles in all. Twenty-eight miles were
through nine inches of deep sand between Cleveland and Akron.
Many miles of soft clay roads were encountered, where wheels
often sank to the axles, and at one point the truck had to ford a
river through two feet of water. From Chicago to Erie, Pennsylvania – some 1,900 miles – it was claimed the truck never
needed to pick up any water, nor was any brake adjustment
required during the entire trip. The tank consumed 355 gallons of
fuel, which averaged 7.1 mpg at an average speed of 16 mph! –
quite an achievement for 1911. Unfortunately, the whole exercise
was overshadowed by the arrival in San Francisco on August 2nd
of a Saurer truck, which had travelled 5,000 miles from New York.

Wyckoff Church & Partridge arranged for the manufacture of
the Commer by W A Wood Auto Manufacturing Co. at Kingston,
NY until Commer themselves set up their own Delaware-registered
company in April 1913. Sales were perhaps the best that any
British model has attained in the US. Americans have always
favoured their home products and this is particularly noticeable in
the trucking industry.

Back home, the Commercial Car was having an unbroken run
of success, added to which the company in June 1909 formed a
subsidiary, Commercial Car Hirers Ltd. The purpose of the latter
company was to offer vehicles, with or without driver, on contract
hire by the hour, day, week, month or year to those needing goods
transported. It was a side of the Commercial Car business at Luton
which had grown steadily since 1907 and now warranted specialised attention. Firms not wanting to tie up capital in motor
vehicles of which they were unsure, found the arrangement ideal,
so did those without a constant need of a motor vehicle, or those
contemplating a bus service and wanting to ascertain the demand
first.

Moore-Brabazon found it convenient to hire a Commer when
he moved his 'new-fangled' flying machine about the country.

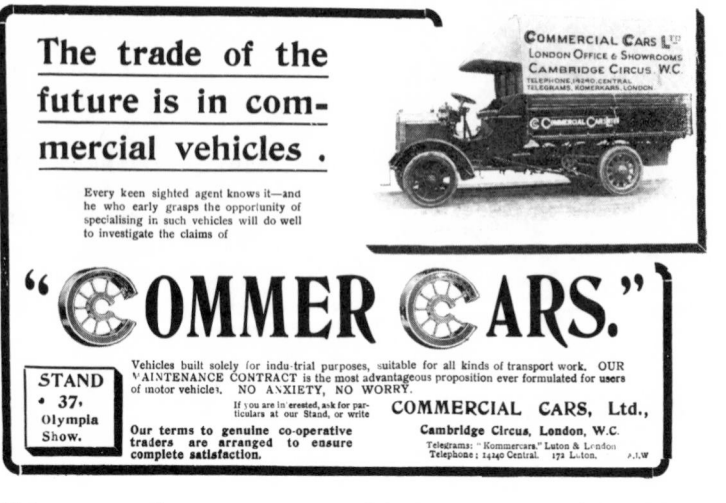

Sixty years ago Commer were aware of the future potential of the truck.
Motor Trader – April 1908

Run from a former horse tramway car shed in Junction Road, Holloway, this business grew to become the major Commer depot in London, also handling spares, repairs and eventually the manufacture of a chassis to be known as the Empire Commercial Vehicle – although this never got off the ground owing to the war.

The Commer did not meet the War Office subsidy requirements, although it was used in special non-combatant duties, such as field workshops, horseboxes, ambulances, etc. Nevertheless, reports of the Commer 'at war' were that they had but a few bad friends. Someone wrote home, mentioning that Lord Northcliffe's former estate Commer had been in France for over a year and no one had put a spanner to it!

The same writer continued, '. . . then I went out to this breakdown Sunday afternoon, nine miles away, and I had a very bad road to travel over, and considering my little BC (Baby Commer) is always carrying 10 cwt overload she did it beautifully. Anyhow, I arrived at where the car was, and found it was a large Rolls-Royce, bedded deeply in a ditch with a broken front axle. We backed my

lorry close up to it and fixed a sling on the two springs, fixed up my derrick blocks and falls and hoisted the car up, fastened it secure and towed it back, up steep hills as well as the bad roads, plus the fact we were overloaded. It was more than we could expect of her, but she did it beautifully. Still she is a Commer, so no more need be said. I am doing a lot of this work and the more she does, the better she goes.'

Commer dropped the Linley pre-selective for the more conventional gearbox and sales after the war seemed to deteriorate slowly. The Humber car firm at Coventry acquired the major shareholding in 1926.

DE DION AND BOUTON

The most renowned name connected with the early automobile in Europe was the French De Dion and Bouton. At the turn of the century the business had the kind of standing that General Motors commands today. De Dion and Bouton had surpassed the sale of 200 cars per month and was well on the way to shipping something like 50,000 loose engines a year. These loose engines went all over the world, usually to other manufacturers of cars who did not have the capital or expertise to make their own. Pierce-Arrow, Peerless and Packard are but three of the American manufacturers who used De Dion engines in their early automobiles.

The De Dion business can be traced back to the early 1880s and is one of the world's first automobile and commercial vehicle manufacturers. In a small Paris suburb, the engineering business of two brothers-in-law, Messieurs Bouton and Trepardoux, was visited one day in 1881 by the Count De Dion. An association formed between the Count and Bouton, but Trepardoux, the senior partner, mistrusted this and left the business a few years later. However, at the outset both partners agreed to work for the Count.

The steam carriage had developed very little in the fifty years since Handcock, Gurney and other early road pioneers, but within a year of the new De Dion partnership, a compact, lightweight, quick-steaming boiler and generator had been constructed: it was to be De Dion's hallmark for the next two decades. Two De Dion-Boutons were entered for the 1897 *Poids Lourds* trials and accomplished one of the most notable performances of the trial.

Having gone through fifteen years or so of traumatic struggle, De Dion manifested itself as *the* automobile business of France. Everything from motorised trikes to tramcars was offered in their catalogue. Steam wagons were almost as important a part of the firm as the sale of motorcars and loose engines. By 1903 their steam buses and wagons were an accepted part of French life, whilst many big cities were using the wagons for refuse collection. The range of light and heavy petrol vans was quite comprehensive

by 1910 and exports, particularly to Britain, were healthy.

Statistics of the period, quoted by Anthony Bird, are impressive. He says that by 1911 the number of employees had risen to over 4,500 and there were reckoned to be more than 50,000 De Dion and Bouton cars in use throughout the world. Moreover, except for tyres, magnetos, ignition coils and various body fitments, all the essential components were made in the company's factory. Taking into account the sales of loose engines to other manufacturers, and those made under licence, the total number of motor cars propelled by De Dion and Bouton machines was not far short of a quarter of a million. This total does not include commercial vehicles or buses, more than 1,000 of the latter were on the streets of Paris, London and New York alone.

Because of the large number of repeat orders from municipal authorities De Dion and Bouton took a keen interest in refuse vehicles as well as buses. A special low-frame chassis was designed which eliminated refuse collectors having to exert themselves by lifting bins too high. These low-frame dustcarts, like the buses, became characterised by the drum-shaped radiator, which was hard to distinguish, except by an expert, from the buses and trucks made by another French concern, Brillie-Schnider.

In 1911 De Dion and Bouton announced they were to enter the luxury car market with a V8-designed engine. Although basically a luxury car, many of these chassis appeared with commercial van and display bodies, whilst during the war a number of these V8s were built in armoured cars.

De Dion's decline was linked to, and many thought was occasioned by the V8, for the car did not appeal to the company's regular clientele. Their lingering demise continued after the war when they dropped the V8 and announced new car and truck models, none of which sold in any quantity. Having been in the forefront of the industry, and because they were rich, De Dion continued to pour their reserves into new models, hoping one of them would catch on, whereas they should, perhaps, have put more enthusiasm into winning back their original customers.

One point that must not be overlooked is that much of De Dion's original success was from the sale of proprietary engines, but these sales merely enabled rival businesses to consolidate their position or to concede defeat and in either case they were not to be customers for De Dion for long.

However, it is to De Dion-Bouton that credit is due for having patented the best drive system ever. To avoid carrying excess

'deadweight' Monsieur Trepardoux designed and patented in 1894 an axle which comprised a tube that took only the unsprung weight of the wheels. The differential was carried on the rear cross member, the propellor shaft being virtually a straight-through drive from the engine – with short cross shafts from the differential to the rear wheels through double universal joints. This design is shown to its greatest advantage with the worm axle and on today's superior roads and road conditions, for the advantage is that it also gives very good road adhesion. Perhaps, therefore, Trepardoux's invention involved more accident than expertise!

DENNIS BROTHERS

Most manufacturers go down in history for having propagated or originated some outstanding design feature; to Dennis goes the honour for the worm and wheel differential. Thought by many at the time to be either too expensive or heavy, the worm won through to become accepted as the best method and has yet to be superseded.

Dennis Brothers is typical of the businesses that found their way into the new motor industry. John Dennis made bicycles from component parts, finding customers with comparative ease at a time when bike riding had become the 'modern wonder'. He opened a cycle store in Guildford soon after Christmas 1894, under the name of Universal Athletic Stores. So popular was the shop with the local youths that John had to call for his younger brother, Raymond, to be his assistant. A logical development was then to motorise the bicycle and De Dion were the people who could be turned to for a good reliable 'loose' engine. So, like the majority of the early motor pioneers, Dennis Brothers set themselves up on the strength of De Dion's good name.

By 1901 Universal Athletic Stores had outstretched the resources of these two young men. Dennis Brothers Limited was registered as a private company with extra finance made available by George Suter and Nicholas Andrew, the latter became Chairman from 1914 and guided the company until 1945. Dennis's first commercial appeared at the Crystal Palace Motor Show – for 1904 – painted and ready for immediate after-show delivery to Harrods store.

The main disadvantage of chain drive was made obvious to London bus operators by the Metropolitan Police. Residents quickly complained that motorbuses gave off noises akin to constant machine gun fire. Thomas Tilling, before purchasing their first motorbus, realised that there was a noise problem and Dennis Brothers, in consultation with Tillings, designed and patented in 1904 (Patent No 3224) their famous worm axle. The worm itself took the form of a three-start thread and, together with the worm wheel and differential gear, was enclosed in a vertically divided casing, similar to a crown and bevel axle – very

Warning:

It having come to our know=
ledge that divers persons are
making and selling, or pro-
pose to make and sell, worm
driving gear and driving axle
connections to Motor Road
Vehicles, in such a way
as to infringe upon our
Letters Patent No. 3224
of 1904, WE HEREBY
GIVE NOTICE that we shall,
upon discovery of any such
infringement, take such steps
to protect our rights as we
may be advised.

DENNIS BROS., LTD., GUILDFORD.

This public warning to the industry appeared in numerous magazines of the
period 1906.

different from the subsequent Dennis 'pot' rear axle introduced in 1913, which had a detachable top casing and the worm shaft over the wheel.

These first worm axles were used by Milnes-Daimler in most of the chassis they sold in the London area – including those sold to Tillings. Dennis Brothers themselves admitted their early worm axles had many teething problems and Tillings found themselves with worm-axle vehicles off the road for at least one in every seven days. Milnes-Daimler decided not to risk their reputation and, for a while, reverted to chains. Another criticism was the alleged irreversibility of the axle. But despite all complaints and problems, Dennis stuck to their belief that the worm was better and won over the market by about 1908. After 1908, other manufacturers saw their wisdom and slowly changed. In the States, once Pierce-Arrow hit the market with worm drive in 1911, within five years the chain was dead.

Dennis Brothers have, of course, been closely associated with fire engines in more recent years. This side of the business grew from 1908 under the guidance of John Downing. Downing came from Fowlers of Leeds in 1902, after having served an apprenticeship in steam. Downing's association with Dennis was known far and wide as he had driven cars in the 1905 Tourist Trophy and 1906 4,000 Mile Reliability Trial. Never more at home than when he was putting new ideas to paper in the drawing office, Downing also supervised the body building shop. He took two engines with turbine pumps to St Paul's and demonstrated to the London County Council the capabilities of Dennis machines. Coupled together, they threw a jet of water right over the dome! When the company became public in 1913 Downing was elected to the Board, but still carried on his active role around the shop floor.

Formation of the public company coincided with Dennis Brothers finally dropping the car side of the business altogether – and the introduction of the new 3-4 ton chassis to War Department standards – with the 'pot' type axle. 7,000 odd trucks were built for the Armed Forces alone.

A prominent feature since 1909 had been the White & Poppe engine and in 1918 Dennis Brothers decided to buy the Coventry-based business in exchange for share capital.

Post-war expansion was directed at the municipal field. Under the lead of Herbert Dowes, who was apprenticed to the company before the war, Dennis Brothers set up a special division to advise on and supply civic bodies with cesspool emptiers, street-watering

and washing machines, gully emptiers and refuse collectors.

Under the misapprehension that hyphenated names impress, Dennis vehicles started to appear during 1923 under the name Dennis-Portland. The name came about with the setting up of a showroom in London's Great Portland Street, whence Dennis Brothers hoped in future to direct all its sales. The name was quickly allowed to fade, although the 2-$2\frac{1}{2}$ ton remained so named for about three years. Lawn mowers, which had become a part of the Dennis catalogue, were where Dennis were lucky enough to be granted the Royal Warrant of Appointment in 1928 – having supplied a motor mower to the Royal Gardens at Windsor. A Royal Warrant was also granted in 1925 for the supplying of a 30 cwt van which was used between Buckingham Palace and Windsor.

The company scored two 'firsts' in London – in 1925 with the first bus to gain Scotland Yard approval with pump-up tyres and in 1926 with the first bus to meet with Scotland Yard approval for 4-wheel brakes.

FODEN

It was a tendency of the early wagon builders to adopt a boiler that was familiar to their already established trade, e.g., Thornycroft and Sentinel, both marine engineers experienced with the vertical boiler, developed their wagons along those lines, with water tubes. Foden, Wallis & Steevens, Mann, Tasker and, in later years, Garrett, Robey, Aveling & Porter and Ransomes, etc, makers of traction engines, clung to the loco-boiler. More general engineers such as Leyland and their antecedents and Coulthard thought in terms of a fire-tube vertical boiler. There is no doubt as to which of the designs would have been best from the customer's viewpoint: the vertical boiler, for it occupied less space. Less non-chargeable space meant more for a paying load. Most potential wagon builders were aware of this fact and, at first, tried their hand at building a vertical boilered wagon. *Building* the *wagon* was not the problem – it was making it work. The vertical boiler had its problems, and how.

Discussing and analysing them could fill a book itself. Those manufacturers like Foden, who were qualified steam men, found themselves embarrassed at their failures with the vertical boiler. To them it became obvious that they should stop wasting time and money (which was valued in those days) on ventures not showing signs of profit. The easy way was to continue along already proven lines – even though they did not exactly fit the customer's requirements. The loco boiler it was to be, and until the Great War this type of wagon was considered the most reliable. Only in very hilly districts did the loco boiler prove difficult to handle: the wagon on a tilt left some parts of the tubes momentarily dry. To solve this particular problem, the younger brother of J H Mann (Mann's Patent Steam Cart & Wagon Company Ltd, Leeds, Yorkshire) designed a boiler to be mounted transversely across the machine. Again the internal politics are too involved, but in brief this was the wagon that eventually became the Yorkshire (illustration 9). Foden, after a troublesome start in the wagon business, ended up at the outset of war with the largest slice of the wagon market. In these early years they never ventured into the petrol engine field

or tried another vertical boiler, that is until much later in life.

However, when the war ended, Sentinel's faith in the undertype was vindicated. The loco boiler was an anachronism and it is sad to recall that there were still a few renowned traction engine builders who had not seen the writing on the wall and ventured into the wagon field at such a late date with loco boilers.

As the twenties drew on it became obvious to nearly all the wagon builders that they had to build undertypes or get out of the business. One by one they all produced their versions, each acclaimed as better than the next. It was no good. Only a few municipalities who did not mind spending other people's money dared invest in untried machines when there was known to be a perfectly good model already – the Sentinel. Foden's sales of the standard loco type that had stood them in good stead for so long were deteriorating. There was no escape they had to develop an undertype or take up the building of petrol machines. For the latter they had not a shred of experience, whereas at least with an undertype they had a chance of salvation. When Foden's undertype – the E model as it was designated – appeared on the market in 1926, the market for steam of any type had further lessened. The day of the steam wagon in Britain was setting. The oil engine was finally to supersede it. Fortunately, Foden saw the light at this point. Their engineers swiftly changed to producing an oiler which was announced to the public in 1931. Foden's obvious lack of enthusiasm for the undertype and their final despondency was reflected in their advertising for the undertype in which they actually stated, 'it is not in the nature of things for an undertype to be superior to the well-established overtype.'

Whilst outside the scope of this edition, it is interesting to recall that the Foden oil-engined lorry was an enormous success. Where Foden left it too late by the twenties to embark upon the undertype field, Sentinel, who continued to do good business even in the late twenties and early thirties, left it too late by the time they came to realise that they should be manufacturing oil engines. Foden had established themselves and Sentinel had no further development by which they could continue to leapfrog.

E B HORNE & CO
GILFORD MOTOR CO LTD

In a small mews opposite London's Royal Northern Hospital in Holloway Road, Mr E B Horne, a builder by trade, purchased, reconditioned and sold war surplus Garford chassis. Horne was bright enough to grasp that the British market lacked a cheap, simple and speedy bus chassis. True, there were the American imported Reos and Chevs, but the British had a resistance to imported chassis, particularly American – and especially so at that time when 'Buy British' was at its zenith.

Buda had not long opened an agency in the Holloway area where they offered the latest 'square' side valve 6-cylinder engine. This was the type of engine that had been popularised in the States by Continental, Buda, Waukesha, Wisconsin, and Lycoming – the top five engine producers in that order.

Horne figured that he could assemble a chassis, made up with a Buda engine. His first appeared, bearing the name Gilford, in May 1925. It closely resembled a Garford 30 cwt chassis and one suspects that the radiator was removed from a Garford. How he struck on the name Gilford is lost in time, but there is no doubt about the close similarity to Garford, which suggests that he merely altered the two letters into something that would resemble Garford, thus trading on some of the goodwill. It has even been suggested that the I and L were initials of a close relative. These Gilford chassis sold – and by the year's end, Horne and his new partner, Mr Victor Skinner, had sold quite a substantial number for a small backyard and unknown assembly firm. Within the year the Gilford name was on the tongue of almost everyone in the trade. Horne and Skinner had designed a new low-frame chassis made at Rubery Owens which was assembled from parts very much to their own specification.

This coach chassis, designated 'Lowline', caught the imagination of the small operators and trade press, and by 1927 was perhaps the most sought-after chassis. Gilfords were not the first in the UK with the low frame. The London General Omnibus Co NS of 1923 was the first and Maudslay offered their version

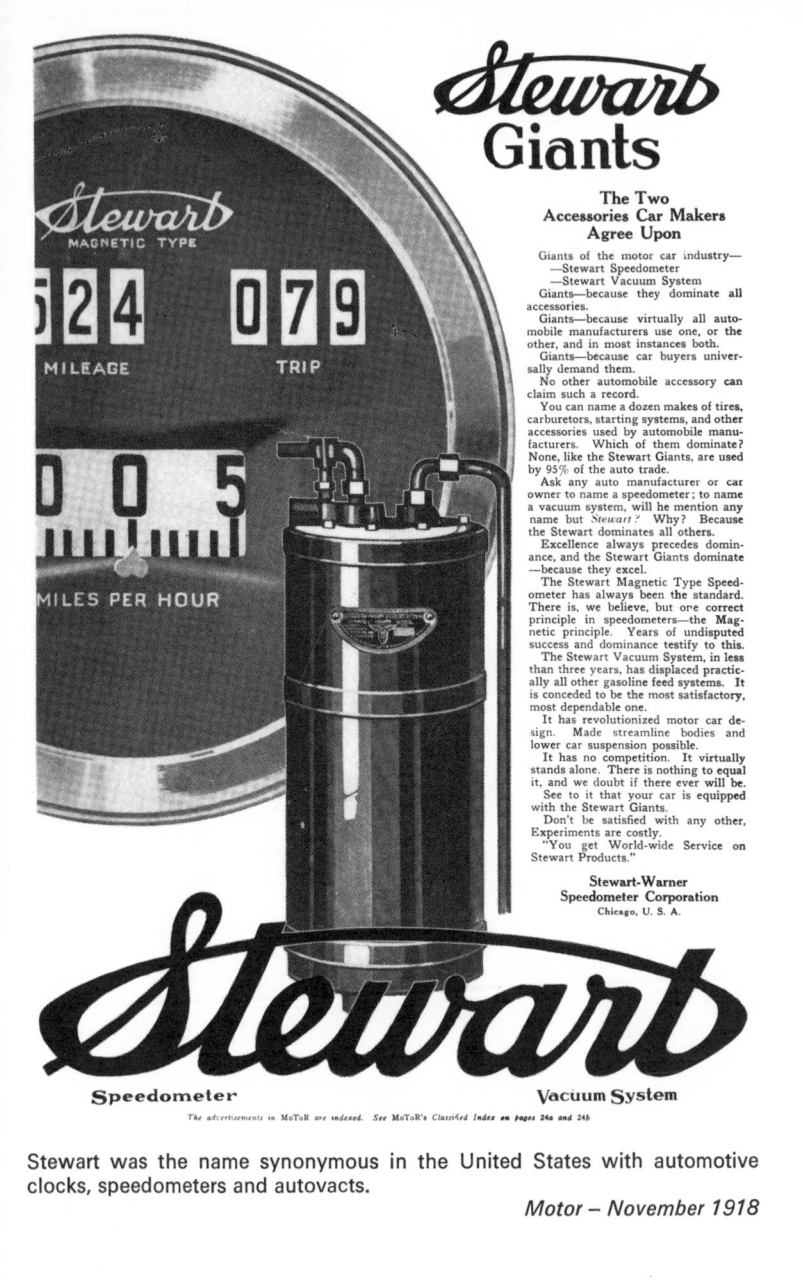

Stewart Giants

The Two Accessories Car Makers Agree Upon

Giants of the motor car industry—
—Stewart Speedometer
—Stewart Vacuum System
Giants—because they dominate all accessories.

Giants—because virtually all automobile manufacturers use one, or the other, and in most instances both.

Giants—because car buyers universally demand them.

No other automobile accessory can claim such a record.

You can name a dozen makes of tires, carburetors, starting systems, and other accessories used by automobile manufacturers. Which of them dominate? None, like the Stewart Giants, are used by 95% of the auto trade.

Ask any auto manufacturer or car owner to name a speedometer; to name a vacuum system, will he mention any name but *Stewart*? Why? Because the Stewart dominates all others.

Excellence always precedes dominance, and the Stewart Giants dominate —because they excel.

The Stewart Magnetic Type Speedometer has always been the standard. There is, we believe, but one correct principle in speedometers—the Magnetic principle. Years of undisputed success and dominance testify to this.

The Stewart Vacuum System, in less than three years, has displaced practically all other gasoline feed systems. It is conceded to be the most satisfactory, most dependable one.

It has revolutionized motor car design. Made streamline bodies and lower car suspension possible.

It has no competition. It virtually stands alone. There is nothing to equal it, and we doubt if there ever will be.

See to it that your car is equipped with the Stewart Giants.

Don't be satisfied with any other. Experiments are costly.

"You get World-wide Service on Stewart Products."

Stewart-Warner
Speedometer Corporation
Chicago, U. S. A.

Stewart

Speedometer   Vacuum System

Stewart was the name synonymous in the United States with automotive clocks, speedometers and autovacts.

Motor – November 1918

early in 1925, but Gilford claimed to be the leaders and were believed. Their assets were cheapness, reliability and speed. Small coach operators found themselves able to afford a chassis on good hire purchase terms, and then run off the road those who were using the sturdier but slower Leylands, Dennises and Tilling-Stevens, etc.

As 1927 drew on Gilfords appeared with Lycoming engines also, and sales had warranted the erection of a new tailor-made factory at High Wycombe, Bucks, which was occupied from Christmas of that year. The Gilford was truly the first British version of the fast inter-city coach which had its roots in America, with the building of the concrete highways, and because of this many people labelled it as an American product.

At the peak of sales around six a week were built and a fair percentage of these were sold as trucks, pantechnicons and vans – the Danish Bacon Company being the largest single purchaser of the vans.

HALLEY

Halley will always be renowned for having been the first to introduce the 6-cylinder engine in a heavy truck chassis onto the British market. George Halley was only a young man of twenty-two when he first started experimenting with his steam wagon. After a year or two experimenting, he formed the Glasgow Motor Lorry Company, which at first continued to build steam wagons, but after another year built both the steam and petrol varieties. The company was reconstructed as a public company in July 1906 with the name Halley's Industrial Motors Ltd. It was four months later that steam was dropped altogether.

Under the direction of George Halley the firm built up an enviable reputation as truck manufacturers north of the border, whence most of their customers emanated. It was early 1920 when Halley first introduced their 6-cylinder chassis onto the market. Six-cylinder engines were, of course, nothing new – they had been used in the more opulent cars since about 1906. And whilst the owners of these expensive cars always bragged about having ample reserve power and cylinders to spare, or to get you home in the event of one or two packing up, users of commercial vehicles put cost before luxury. Extra cylinders meant extra petrol and added running costs. They also meant loss of payload space, for the early 6-cylinder engines were long. The 6-cylinder was, though, smoother running than the four, it balanced more easily, and impulses being more frequent the torque was more even. These advantages were to be realised once the city to city expressways had been constructed in the States. Then, of course, there arose a need to develop a 6-cylinder engine for express coaches. The engines, however, had to be smaller and certainly on one-piece block casting.

Halley realised the potential of the 6-cylinder engine, especially its smooth running over long distances. Unfortunately, instead of developing a monobloc engine they rushed into the market with a 35 hp engine cast in two blocks of three. The engine took up a lot of space – was expensive to run and confirmed all the fears of any commercial operator of the period. It was slow to catch on.

George Halley, who was the guiding force behind the company, died in 1921 and without him the company floundered. Halley's 6-cylinder engine was never fully developed in the way that it ought to have been, but within a couple of years 6-cylinder engines had started to appear in earnest in the States. The lightweight, monobloc unit with closely spaced small-bore cylinders and side valves proved to be cheap to produce and the most efficient engine, being not only simple in construction but also for maintenance. It was the engine that hallmarked nearly every American bus and truck from about 1927 and had a good deal of popularity in Britain and Europe.

Unfortunately, whilst Halley were able to see many of the advantages of the 6-cylinder and pioneered the principle, they never shared in any of the profits when the fashion was at its zenith, for Halley went into voluntary liquidation in 1926 and the factory building was absorbed by another Scottish manufacturer of commercial vehicles – Albion Motors.

LACRE

A British name so rarely heard today and almost certainly non-existent in the mind of the public is Lacre. Yet Lacre was, at one time, a leading name and today is as important as ever – only their activities are now concentrated not on chassis construction but municipal cleansing equipment, built on other manufacturers' chassis.

The name Lacre was a contraction of Long Acre, a main thoroughfare through London's Covent Garden market, where the company's founder, Claude Brown, started in the automobile business. Their place in Long Acre did not last long, for by 1904, when the firm made its first commercial, they had a factory in Poland Street. Poland Street is close to Oxford Circus and even in those days was an unusual place to build vehicles. Even so, this probably accounted for Lacre's early success, which was selling light vans to the leading London stores, such as Shoolbred, Peter Robinson, Thomas Wallis, Harrods and Whiteleys. In fact, Shoolbred was where Lacre secured their first success, perhaps with the knowledge that if anything went wrong or was needed, the factory was within walking distance. The stores put a great deal of faith in Lacre. Lacre vans soon held a prominent place in the growing delivery business that was offered to the outskirts of London and the Home County towns resulting from the reliability of the motor van. They quickly became known to other leading firms of the day – Berry's Boot Polish, Bryant & May's Matches, Hedges & Butler, Carter Paterson and the Cooperative Society Ltd. It should be noted that although Lacre did build their own vehicles in Poland Street, the first couple of years production was, in fact, made at the Albion Works in Scotstown, Glasgow, and bore an uncanny resemblance to the Albion. Lacre were indeed sole concessionaires in England and Wales for the Albion, and London agents for Wolseley and Siddeley. Likewise, arrangements were made within a year or so with another business to market their products as well – the new business being the Hammersmith-based James & Browne. They offered a rather odd 2-cylinder engine van, which had a transverse crankshaft and

flywheels between the cylinders, the driver sitting over the engine. Lacre called these the J B Lacre and they sold well, alongside the normal range.

The time soon came when Lacre had outgrown the Poland Street factory, and they chose to have a factory built in the new 'dream town' of Letchworth, Hertfordshire. Letchworth was the first of the garden cities, built on the conception of ideal conditions for people to live and work. Lacre claimed this new factory at Letchworth was the first in the country to be designed and built especially for the manufacture of commercial vehicles.

No sooner had they moved into the factory in the summer of 1910 than they offered to the market an idea that could have saved pounds in labour costs and hours of frustration. No longer was it necessary to get out and get under – with Lacre's new design the entire engine pulled out like a cabinet drawer. It was a revolution in England, but not in America.

In America it was a style associated with the Grabowsky truck, designed by Max Grabowsky in 1902. The Grabowsky trucks were popular for their ease of accessibility, but not popular enough to avoid financial disaster in 1912. All the Grabowsky tools were acquired from the Receiver by the Seitz Automobile & Transmission Company at Wyandotte, Michigan, who carried on building trucks with this innovation under the model name Homer. Progressive ideas never seem to win the day, for the Homer did not last long and Lacre sold none. Morris Commercial tried to revive the design in the late twenties but only today is it a prominent feature of London's famous Routemaster buses.

By the war, the mainstay of the Lacre production line was a $2-2\frac{1}{2}$ tonner, referred to as the O-type. The Belgian Army ordered forty of these at the outset of war and so impressed were the Belgians with the prompt delivery that they purchased Lacre's entire output for the next two years. During the war Lacre also designed and supplied to the Belgians various special pieces of equipment, including a pontoon. For this, and general appreciation of Lacre, the Belgian Government decorated the company's Chief Engineer, Mr J S Drewry.

A market that had escaped manufacturers, including Lacre, who by accident stumbled across the idea, was supplying mechanical road sweepers to municipalities. Street sweepers until then had been crude adaptations of private car or ordinary truck chassis. Lacre's first sweeper was an adaptation of the O-type chassis, made to special order in 1917, and this prompted them to design a

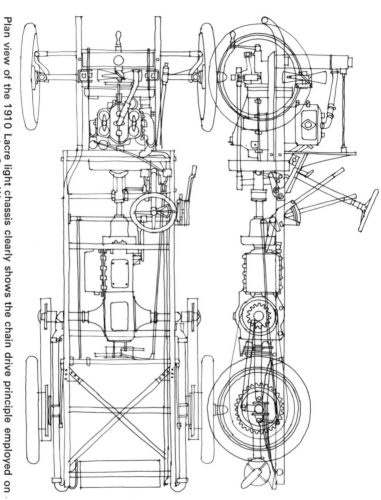

Plan view of the 1910 Lacre light chassis clearly shows the chain drive principle employed on most commercials until the Great War.

custom-built chassis for the purpose. When it appeared in 1919 it offered a tremendous step forward over what municipalities had been using. Lacre's L-type sweeper was not only inexpensive to buy and economical to operate – it did the job magnificently. Its single, steered rear wheel meant it could get the broom into the most difficult places – it had a small turning circle, whilst the broom gave a good width of sweep.

This road sweeper was to be Lacre's salvation for many years, little though the firm knew it at the time. When the war ended, the general recession hit the truck manufacturers harder because of the vast number of cheap war surplus trucks. Whereas Lacre had difficulty getting orders for their trucks, sales for the sweeper from the municipalities were regular. To add to Lacre's problems their brilliant Chief Engineer, J S Drewry, responsible for much of Lacre's good reputation, left in 1922 to start a rival business, Shelvoke & Drewry, in the municipal field. Shelvoke & Drewry, whose business was also in Letchworth, entered the market the following year with a low-chassis freighter (Illustration Nos 122/3).

The supplying of mechanical road sweepers was not enough to sustain the vast factory and staff at Letchworth, and Lacre's financial position gradually deteriorated until late 1927, when, after an abortive attempt to amalgamate with Walker Brothers (Wigan) Ltd (Manufacturers of the Pagefield truck), Lacre declared itself bankrupt. In January 1928 a new company was formed, reviving the Lacre name and continuing with sweeper production, but on premises more suited to the company's demand.

LANCASHIRE STEAM MOTORS LTD
LEYLAND MOTORS LTD

'If we don't make this firm a success now, we deserve to be kicked. We've got the world by the pants and a downhill pull!' Such were the words uttered by Henry Spurrier 'the Second' to William Sumner after coming away with the first prize at the 1897 self-propelled vehicles trials in Manchester.

Britain's first manufacturer to concentrate entirely on the production of commercial vehicles is today the dominant partner in the UK's largest automobile manufacturing organisation: the British Leyland Motor Corporation. The history of Leyland can be traced back to the days of the Industrial Revolution, where in the village of Leyland, Lancashire, the Sumner family possessed and handed down from generation to generation a small foundry business. James Sumner, who inherited the business in 1892, was dedicated to making self-propelled wagons and had built a steam-driven wagon in 1884 which gave service to a local coalman for a year or so. Photographs or drawings of the wagon have yet to come to light, but in their absence it may be assumed that this was the world's second self-propelled machine designed to carry goods.

James Sumner and his younger brother, William, continued to experiment with the steam engine, mounted first to a tricycle and later to a lawn-mower. This steam lawn-mower won first prize at the Royal Lancashire Agricultural Show, virtually guaranteeing the Lancashire steam lawn-mower further sales. In fact, steam lawn-mowers became the backbone of the business for some five or six years.

The Sumner business was in need of extra capital and after a brief fifty-fifty stock ownership with T Coulthard, a business in Preston also interested in steam wagons, Sumner met up with the wealthy Spurrier family. From this association came the formation of the Lancashire Steam Motor Company in 1896, the name being changed to Leyland Motors Ltd in 1907.

In addition to James Sumner, three Spurriers became directors: Henry, a retired businessman, known as 'Henry the First', Henry Spurrier 'the Second', and George. The new company wasted no

time in building an oil-fired steam van which in 1897 participated in the Royal Agricultural Society self-propelled vehicles trials at Manchester, where it won first prize and occasioned the ebullient statement mentioned above. Henceforth, the small Leyland business never turned back. Financial problems it may have had over the years but the level-headed, astute business sense that characterises so many Lancastrians has continued to prevail.

Only at brief intervals has the firm diversified from commercials to curiosities like petrol-electric tramcars and motorcars, and these two breakaways were both to appease the firm's Chief Engineer, Parry Thomas, whose ideas they were. This holding to one line is greatly to Leyland's credit. Many manufacturers in their lean times have thought the grass greener on the other side and opted to make cars, or vice versa, only to find out that it wasn't the market that was at fault but their own product or skill. The first petrol-engined vehicle of 1904 was not a success. Leylands knew the art of steam; petrol was foreign to them and they fell into all the pitfalls obvious to today's engineers and, no doubt, to motor-minded men of the time. Leylands saw their problems and acted by entering into an agreement with the Manchester engineering firm of Crossley Motors.

Leyland was not a great company even in 1907, as witness the sales figures for the year: thirty-six steamers and seventeen petrols, but each one that left the factory could be said to be of the highest calibre and the company went to great lengths to guarantee its name should a vehicle break down.

As the years led up to the war, Leyland offered a choice of two basic types which varied as subsequent modifications were made. Up to three tons, Leyland recommended their 24 or 30 hp cab-over-engine model, very popular with local councils. Between three and five tons, the bonneted 40 hp, which later became the basis of the Subsidy A type lorry. After five tons, Leyland considered steam the best proposition. Leyland really claimed to be impartial as builders of both steam and petrol vehicles and they certainly laid down no hard and fast rules, for customers could, if they wished, buy 4 and 5-ton cab-over-engines or 2-ton bonneted vehicles.

The governments of both Germany and France had seen the possibilities of motor transport in times of war and set up subsidy schemes as early as 1906. The idea was not that the government should invest public money, buying machines that were either no good or outmoded if war did come. The government would give a

grant to purchasers so that if hostilities commenced they could be called upon. The Germans started to lay down firm stipulations as to how the vehicles should be built in order to qualify from 1908. The British were much slower in such matters. British generals, having fought wars since time immemorial failed to see the importance of the motor vehicle and thought that any future wars would be fought with horses – even at the height of the First World War some generals still refused to believe that it was the first war of mechanical trial and strength.

Various War Office trials had been organised from 1901, and in 1908 the War Office started a subsidy scheme for traction engines. In 1911 the government announced a scheme for motor vehicles, divided into two classes, 'A' for 3-ton loads, and 'B' for 30 cwt. In its wisdom, the government, with virtually no experience, and a military composed of men with even less interest in motor vehicles, proceeded to lay down specifications to manufacturers and operators so that they could be eligible for a subsidy of between £8–£12 with a £15 subsidy thereafter; a mere pittance compared with the subsidies offered in Germany and France. The subsidy was raised in 1914 to £120, payable in four instalments over three years.

The Leyland 3-tonner became the mainstay of the Subsidy 'A' type scheme. When war broke out in August 1914 those manu-facturers accepted for subsidy were Dennis, Hallford, Karrier, Maudsley, Thornycroft and Wolseley in addition to Leyland. As the war drew on, W F Bradley, reporting firsthand, said the British subsidy trucks were a poor job compared with their American and French counterparts. The British government had laid down such uniform specifications that the faults, instead of showing up in only one make, repeated themselves in all of them. Reviewing the situation, he commented that the French trucks were best – the French had been wise. Whatever type of vehicle steam, gas, gas-electric, or whichever drive system – the subsidy applied. All that was required was for the truck to be capable of doing a good job of work.

The best British vehicle, the London General Omnibus Com-pany B-type bus chassis, was strangely enough not one of the subsidized types. Whilst government repair manuals of the period listed long series of modifications for WD lorries, only one suggestion could be offered for the B (not a compulsory one at that) – the compression of the engine should be lowered.

At the War's end, 165,128 vehicles were in the possession of the

War Department, 66,352 of which were lorries, Leyland's portion of that amount being 6,411 or 10%. The majority of these vehicles would eventually be sold by public auction, flooding the market with cheaply priced trucks and further adding to the recession in firms' sales at a time when the country was entering a slump period. Leyland recognised the potential danger of an unlimited surplus of trucks, and the bad reputation they could acquire if the vehicles were not up to standard. With this in mind, they negotiated with the War Department to repurchase all the Leylands not too far from home, which amounted to 3,111. From the government, the former Sopwith Aviation Company hangar at Ham, near Kingston-upon-Thames was purchased and in this new division of Leyland Motors the rebuilding of almost every one of the 3,111 Leylands was undertaken. After overhaul, they were offered on the market alongside new Leyland vehicles selling at £1,050 each, the last leaving the Ham factory late in January 1926. These reconditioned trucks gave remarkable service in their later life, some lasting until the early 1950s, trundling around London working for such firms as Maples and Waring & Gillow, who had been purchasers of the original Leyland subsidy chassis forty years earlier.

Despite the enormous capital costs tied up in repurchasing these trucks, together with the general recession, Leyland somehow survived some of the most difficult years of this century. Their low ebb came in the years 1926–1927, by which time they had recouped their capital. They had no new designs to offer those customers prepared to pay the full market price and, of course, they had exhausted the cheaper line for those that could not afford a new truck – the latter being a large slice of the market in those days.

But the lean days were not to last for long. The brilliant young engineer who had served his training in the LGOC/AEC drawing office before the war, G J Rackham, had emigrated to the United States, but now decided to return to his homeland. Back in England he took up the position of Chief Engineer at Leyland in 1927. Finding that their whole range was outmoded by more than a decade, he designed an entirely new range of vehicles based on his American expertise. Bus versions were the first to be on view at the Olympia Commercial Show in November and these were to prove a turning point in Leyland's history, giving the company back its pre-war status as Britain's leading commercial vehicle producer.

MACK BROTHERS

No other name can surely be more synonymous with the US truck industry than Mack. 'Built like a Mack' is still a phrase used by Americans to signify something solid or sturdy. This slogan came in during the First World War, but long before then the Mack trucks proved to be of the sturdiest quality Americans could wish for.

The Mack story begins when John M Mack and his brother, Augustus, purchased a wagon builder's shop in Brooklyn. In 1900 they built a very advanced-looking 20-seat char-a-banc to order for sightseeing in and around the neighbourhood's Prospect Park. The success of this 'chara' was enough for Jack Mack and his brothers (there were three others besides Augustus) to discard the wagon business in favour of the manufacture of more buses and trucks. Jack, though, was the strong-willed leader of the family. Under his direction the business was assembling trucks, buses and cars of reputable quality within a few years – and they were being sold with ease. The small wagon shop in Brooklyn was soon outgrown and there was enough capital for enlarged premises. Brother Joseph, a silk grower in Pennsylvania's Allentown, convinced Jack and the other brothers that the new plant should be outside New York on the grounds that land and labour were more plentiful, and they would be nearer to the rich markets developing in Philadelphia, Pittsburgh and other cities further west. Macks made the move in 1906 and have, from that day, never looked back. Macks only concern was lest their name should be forgotten in and around New York once they departed, so they named their trucks after the city – henceforth they were to be marketed as Manhattans. The change was not needed, however, for it was proved that the Mack name had a greater reputation than their makers believed, and the name Manhattan was used only for a short while on the bigger trucks.

In the Autumn of 1911, Mack Brothers entered into an agreement with a new Wall Street backed syndicate, International Motor Company, whereby the latter took over the marketing and after-sales servicing. The International Motor Company, set up

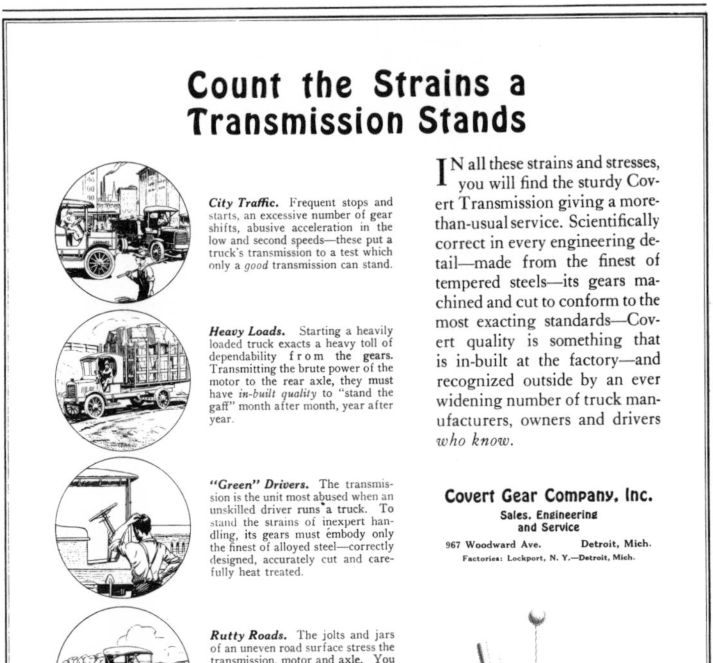

Count the Strains a Transmission Stands

City Traffic. Frequent stops and starts, an excessive number of gear shifts, abusive acceleration in the low and second speeds—these put a truck's transmission to a test which only a *good* transmission can stand.

Heavy Loads. Starting a heavily loaded truck exacts a heavy toll of dependability from the gears. Transmitting the brute power of the motor to the rear axle, they must have *in-built quality* to "stand the gaff" month after month, year after year.

"Green" Drivers. The transmission is the unit most abused when an unskilled driver runs a truck. To stand the strains of inexpert handling, its gears must embody only the finest of alloyed steel—correctly designed, accurately cut and carefully heat treated.

Rutty Roads. The jolts and jars of an uneven road surface stress the transmission, motor and axle. You demand a *proven* motor and axle in the truck you buy; make sure that the transmission is of an equally dependable make—proven by performance.

IN all these strains and stresses, you will find the sturdy Covert Transmission giving a more-than-usual service. Scientifically correct in every engineering detail—made from the finest of tempered steels—its gears machined and cut to conform to the most exacting standards—Covert quality is something that is in-built at the factory—and recognized outside by an ever widening number of truck manufacturers, owners and drivers *who know.*

Covert Gear Company, Inc.
Sales, Engineering and Service
967 Woodward Ave. Detroit, Mich.
Factories: Lockport, N. Y.—Detroit, Mich.

COVERT
TRANSMISSION

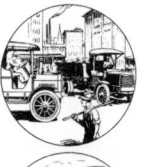

By the late teens American trucks 'built-up' of component parts were becoming the order of the day. Covert were among the first compact transmission manufacturers to offer ball-change for heavy vehicles.

Motor – January 1918

under Delaware laws, had a share capital of $10,000,000. Its directors, made up mainly of bankers, also included representatives of the American Car & Foundry Company and the American Brake, Shoe & Foundry Company, whilst Jack Mack became Vice President. The presidency was taken by Mr C P Colman, president of the American concession owners of the Swiss Saurer Motor Company. This concession also entered into a similar agreement with the new syndicate, and within a few months was joined by the Hewitt Motor Co.

The new consortium hoped to sell 2,000 trucks in its first year but was dismayed when only 1,150 had been sold by the end of 1912. IMC declared to its shareholders that it lacked working capital and asked for dividends to be loaned to the company.

Meanwhile, Jack Mack had been taking a personal interest in electric vehicles and acquired control of the Lansden Company in Newark, New Jersey, from Thomas Edison in May 1912. Lansden were one of the firms who promoted the 'trolley-lorry' idea shown in the illustration.

In the Spring of 1913 John Calder, formerly Associate General Manager of Cadillac, took on the job of supervising the engineering and design of all Mack, Saurer and Hewitt trucks, greatly to the annoyance of Edward Hewitt. Hewitt had been unhappy at the new consortium but had agreed to act as Consultant Engineer to IMC. One of his arguments had been that IMC was formed with the idea of picking the industry's best brains – Hewitt's included.

Though it was not foreseen when the firm unveiled its new design, the AC model, in 1915, the Mack name was to be immortalised in history. The ugly, square-nosed AC model was as tough as it looked – and it looked as though it had been cut out of a solid block of steel. When they got to US Army service in Europe, the 'dough-boys' found they resembled the British 'bulldog' character – they kept going whatever the consequences and were untiring in their role, so the AC model and its derivates up to 1939 were simply Bulldog Macks to everybody.

Sadly, Jack Mack at the age of sixty was involved in an accident with a Lehigh Valley Transit Interurban trolley car whilst at the wheel of his Chandler on March 14, 1920. He died instantly.

M.A.N.

A late starter among the heavy truck producers was MAN (Maschinenfabrik Augsburg-Nurnberg). This old-established manufacturer of stationary engines was directed by the German government to build the Swiss 5-ton Saurer truck under licence in 1915. MAN had for many years had a relationship with Saurer. Way back in the 1890s, MAN helped Dr Rudolf Diesel make a working oil engine. Intermittently between 1898 and 1912 efforts were made jointly by MAN and Saurer to apply the oil engine to a road vehicle, and an air-blast injection engine was shown by MAN at Turin in 1911. But Dr Diesel could not make the air-blast injection work and had failed to perfect any other way of injecting the fuel.

After the war MAN decided to remain in the truck business. The acute petrol crisis in Germany at that time was, no doubt, an additional factor in MAN's decision to continue with their efforts to resolve the injection problem. A solution was found by Bursch, who were able to develop fuel injection parts and make them available at prices that were acceptable enough to make the oil engine a commercial proposition.

The oil engine theory was now beginning to be appreciated by a number of engineers and operators. If the engine could be perfected it would quarter the running costs of a vehicle with, say, a petrol engine consuming 4–6 mpg. Even in those years of reasonably cheap petrol, 4–6 mpg could add quite a fuel bill to the weekly budget. For this reason alone many firms were prepared to spend considerable time and money developing the oil engine.

MAN naturally stole the lead by exhibiting a workable 45 hp 5 litre engine suitable for a truck of 3-ton load capacity, at the December 1924 Berlin Motor Show: at 1500 rpm it was considered a high-speed engine. The Bavarian Post Office were the first to come forward and demonstrate their faith by ordering the engine from MAN. Despite the advanced look of the chassis, disc clutch and gearbox, mounted in unit with the engine – it was chain driven.

Henceforth, MAN and Saurer went on to maintain their lead

for several years and by 1932 MAN had discontinued *all* their petrol range.

The British, who had lagged well behind, perhaps because they favoured the steam wagon which was equally cheap with its home-burnt fuel, sat up and took a hard look at the oiler in 1928. That was the year the Dewar Challenge Trophy was unexpectedly awarded to C B Wardman for covering 700 miles in a Benz oil lorry and trailer of 12 tons with a fuel consumption of $13\frac{1}{2}$ mpg!

Whilst MAN were able to offer a powerful enough engine in their 6–10 ton range by 1931, it took another year or two, including a great deal of headache and frustration, before other manufacturers could get the oil engine to near perfection. By then it could haul the heaviest of loads and formed the final nail in the coffin of the steam wagon.

MOTOR OMNIBUS CONSTRUCTION LTD (MOC)
ASSOCIATED EQUIPMENT CO. LTD (AEC)
ASSOCIATED DAIMLER CO. LTD (ADC)

The need of every manufacturer is for experience: how his product is performing, how good a service it gives, and how it can be improved upon. Ideally, every manufacturer needs to be the operator in order to have the information first hand.

The founder of the London Motor Omnibus Company, Salisbury-Jones, and his co-directors, among whom was Sir Armstrong-Whitworth, were quick to realise this; only they were operators and not manufacturers. The experience the newly-formed London Motor Omnibus Company (fleet name, *Vanguard*) was to acquire, was to be used in assisting the company to build their own vehicles to their own specific needs. Consequently, the London Motor Omnibus Company directors formed a new associated concern, the Motor Omnibus Construction Company. Within weeks they acquired ground at Walthamstow, had a factory erected, and the first chassis were being assembled from component parts. Items for special requirements were manufactured under the direction of the appointed Chief Engineer, Mr R Turner-Smith. The engines came from the Lincolnshire traction engine firm of R Hornsby & Sons, whilst the axles were the product of the Newcastle factory of Armstrong-Whitworth.

The first few chassis appeared in 1906, painted in the livery of yet another London Motor Omnibus Company associate, the London & Provincial Motor Omnibus Company (fleet name, *Pilot*). What happened afterwards is a mystery. Records fail to show if the chassis was a success or a failure, or even how many were made. The MOC looked identical to another make that made an appearance between 1907 and 1911 – the Armstrong-Whitworth. The technical press often referred to MOCs as Armstrong-Whitworths and *vice versa*. No doubt Sir Armstrong-Whitworth's influence on the board of MOC had a great deal to do with this. One fact is clear, the Salisbury-Jones empire was in financial trouble at the start of 1907, which resulted in the amalgamation of

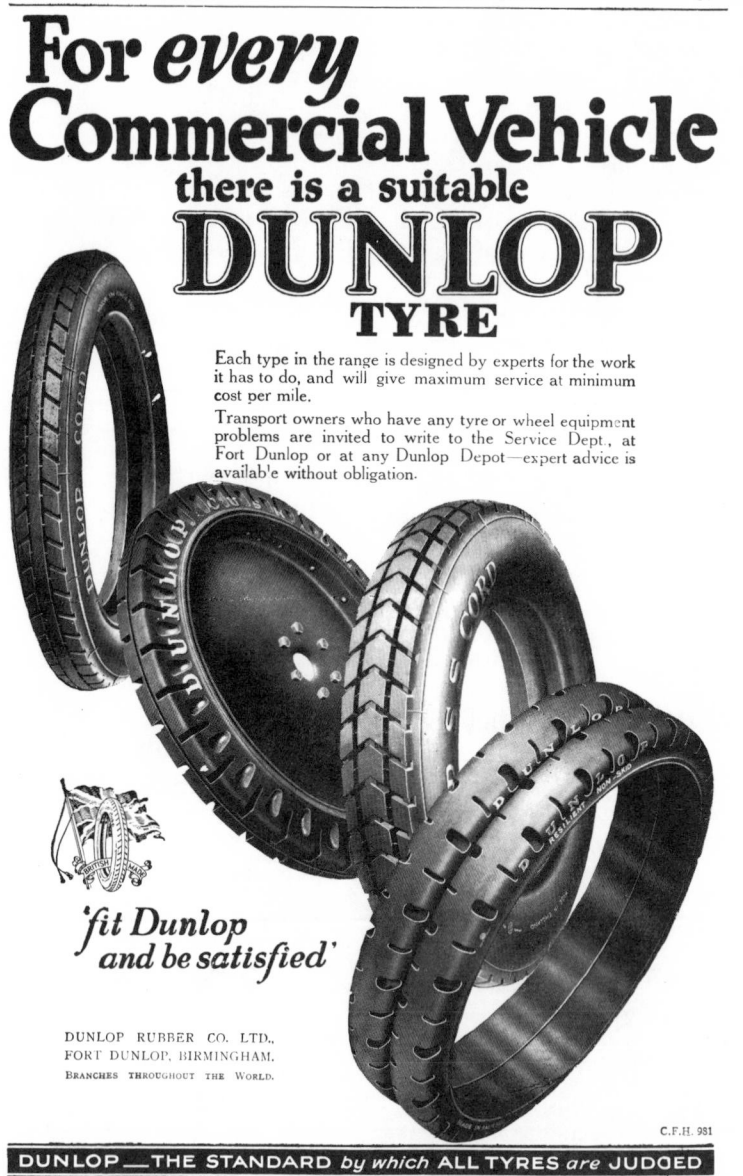
Please mention the "World's Carriers Year Book" when replying to Advertisements.

Dunlop Tyres – popular then as they are today.

Worlds Carriers Year Book 1926

all the various operating companies into one, the Vanguard Motor Omnibus Company. The merger made little difference to the finances though. Whilst Vanguard had been (and still was) doing rewarding business, they lacked the reserves needed to stabilise such a new and vast operation. The London General Omnibus Company on the other hand, was long established, the second largest bus concern in London with considerable reserves, which were being eaten into by the sudden losses incurred by motor bus competition. Vanguard thus decided to do no more experimentation at MOC, but used the Walthamstow factory as a central repair and experimental shed.

The finances of the London General Omnibus Company, the Vanguard Omnibus Company and another well-established horse bus concern, the London Road Car Company (trading as *Union Jack*) were all merged in July 1908. The outcome of this union was an immediate fusion of LGOC money and Vanguard talent. At the Vanguard company were perhaps some of the best motorbus engineers in Britain, including a young man in the drawing office by the name of G J Rackham, who in later years revolutionized both Leyland AEC's designs.

The first job of the new concern, which carried on the London General Omnibus Company name, was to produce a reliable vehicle to their own specifications and requirements. The outcome was a 34-seat bus, known as the X-type, of which sixty-one were built. This chassis bore a remarkable resemblance to the earlier MOC. Then in November 1910 the LGOC announced its new and improved X-type – the 'B'. The 'B' was built on a flitched wood/steel frame with worm drive and chain gearbox, supporting a 34-seat body with an overall weight of $3\frac{1}{2}$ tons. It proved an immediate success. The LGOC increased the original order and within a year all the company's horse buses had been made redundant.

In 1912 the Underground group of companies headed by Mr Albert Stanley (later Lord Ashfield) purchased the majority of the LGOC shares and under new direction the Walthamstow manufacturing side was turned into a separate concern, the Associated Equipment Company with Albert Stanley as Chairman. The 'B' chassis continued to be made only for LGOC requirements, but by 1913 surplus chassis were being made available to the Daimler Company, which would act as sales agent. The announcement that the AEC was to be on the open market brought a sharp rebuke from other manufacturers in the industry, frightened that the

LGOC was now about to saturate the provinces with bus chassis at cost. Fears were, however, groundless for few chassis were sold outside London before the war. When the war came, a quarter of the LGOC fleet was requisitioned and shipped to France where it was put to various uses. Now the government approached AEC with the purpose of supplying lorry chassis to their requirements. As AEC had only built the flitched plate B chassis, it meant that under the direction of their new young Chief Engineer, Charles K Edwards, they had to manufacture a chassis along the lines of the requirements laid down by the government's subsidy scheme. The first-off all-steel chassis appeared in 1915 in the guise of B-type single-deck buses (Nos 2679–2708). Thereafter, the steel-framed lorries were to be known as Y-types, although many earlier lorries built for the War Department had flitched chassis and were, in fact B-types with chassis numbers in sequence with those built for the LGOC. At the war's end, the AEC factory had been greatly enlarged and was ready to produce not only a new bus chassis for the LGOC but to buy back many of the WD lorries, recondition and resell them, and build lorries and buses in quantity for the open market at last. Charles K Edwards remained as Chief Engineer, designing the LGOC's first post-war bus chassis, the K-type, within six months from the earliest drawing board stage to the completed prototype. The K was London's first successful cab-S-type did, due to the requirements of the LGOC, who considered this method of construction lighter and more flexible. The new post-war goods chassis, aside from the 5-ton Y-type, was the 2-ton model announced in 1922.

In 1926 Lord Ashfield made arrangements with the Daimler Company at Coventry, whereby the two firms combined their selling divisions and their technical knowledge. A new Associated Daimler Company offered a wide range of chassis from the Coventry and Walthamstow factories with AEC 4-cylinder engines or Daimler 6-cylinder sleeve valve engines. This later engine was that which Daimler's Chief Engineer, Lawrence Pomeroy, was using in the firm's private car range. This led to numerous heated arguments between the AEC design staff, who bitterly opposed putting a car engine into a bus or truck chassis. However, Pomeroy refused to accept that the truck and bus range needed a specially designed engine and so were sown the seeds of a break in the relationship – to come after 1927.

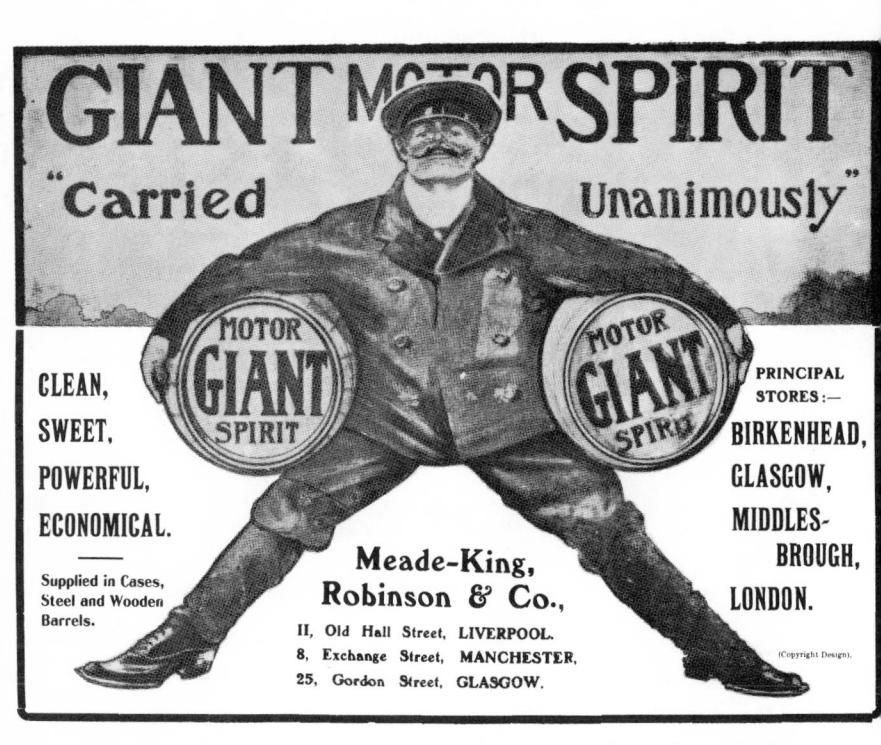

Giant motor spirit were absorbed in the Shell combine just prior to the Great War.

Commercial Motor – October 1905

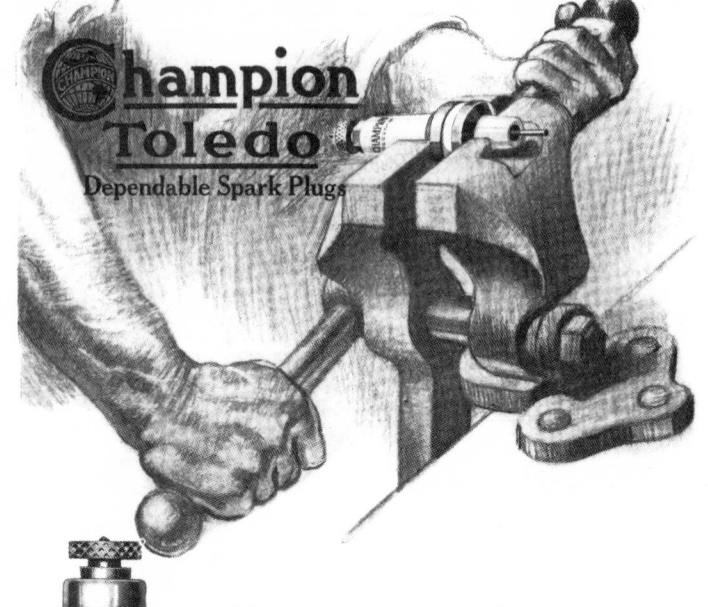

Champion Toledo
Dependable Spark Plugs

IF YOU put your spark plugs in a vise and exerted all your strength to subject them to the greatest possible pressure, you would expect the porcelain to crumble.

Yet that's virtually what they must stand in your motor.

As you get under way, the explosions in your cylinders become so rapid that the force they exert is practically continuous.

In Champion-Toledo Dependable Spark Plugs, the shoulders of the porcelain insulators are cushioned against this tremendous pressure.

The two patented copper gaskets that protect the porcelain where the pressure comes are lined with asbestos so that the metal cannot touch the porcelain.

That's one reason why Champions are so much more durable and dependable than ordinary spark plugs.

Get the Champion-Toledo Plug designed to serve your kind of motor (your dealer or garage man knows which one) and you have assured maximum efficiency and durability.

Be sure that the name "Champion" is on the porcelain—not merely on the box.

CHAMPION
REG. U.S. PAT. OFF.

Heavy Stone for High
Powered Cars, $1.25

Champion Spark Plug Company, Toledo, Ohio

One name has not disappeared in all the mergers – Champion, leaders in the sale of plugs.

.Motor – February 1918

PACKARD AUTOMOBILE COMPANY

The word is pronounced *Packerd* by native Americans, whilst the British insist the 'a' is there to be sounded. The origins of this firm are typical of my observations in the preface. One school of thought is that, before the turn of the century, James Ward Packard ordered a Winton car, then the best available, and was furious when the car was delivered new to his house, towed by a horse after having broken down. Packard demanded the car be put right or his money back. Winton refused on both points, whereupon Packard replied that he would build a car and show Winton what the world's best car should be like. He did just that. He then went on to build up the business, but sold out his share fairly quickly, after completing his mission, which was to prove Winton a poor engineer.

The story perpetuated by other historians and the company is that Packard was anxious to build his own car as early as 1890 and, in fact, had ideas 'on paper' for a vehicle of some sort by 1893. No doubt there is some truth in both stories. Packard probably had some secret longing, but never got around to practical work until jogged along by his brush with Winton. No doubt, also, Packard being a gentleman, he didn't mention the Winton incident except to close friends, and certainly it would have been bad company public relations for Packard to issue histories saying the company had been started because its founder wanted to spite another manufacturer!

Whatever the truth of the matter, it was in 1899 that James Ward Packard and his brother, W D, started the Ohio Automobile Company in Warren, Ohio, changing the company's name to Packard in 1902 and moving to Detroit, Michigan in 1903. During these years Packard built up a modest business, producing 'quality' automobiles – not that this was unusual. Until Henry Ford most people thought that the automobile market could only ever be for the rich.

Packard's involvement in the truck market in 1905 was nothing spectacular. In those years the truck was still considered to be a novelty, even if private automobiles were accepted in some circles.

Manufacturers came and went by the dozen, many producing one truck, others only a lot of drawings and stock exchange prospectuses. Companies were not fighting one another so much as a public attitude of mind. US trucks of 1905 were little more than modified private car chassis, or they were electric. Steam in the States just never won over.

It wasn't until 1909 that Packard could be said to have gone down in 'folklore' as making any serious contribution to the truck industry. The Americans accepted without question a set formula for designing trucks. The driver sat over the engine. The Americans had no doubts that not only did the driver have greater facility for handling the vehicle in heavy traffic with this method, but less space was wasted, lower fuel cost and maintenance was afforded, and a near even distribution of load possessed a further advantage in relieving the rear springs, axles, wheels, bearings and tyres of some of the inherent side thrust. In the UK and Europe, the exact opposite was thought. Cab-over-the-engine was putting too much weight on the front axle, it caused excessive tyre and axle wear, it was said. Even Karriers of Huddersfield agreed and thought the only advantage was better driver vision – yet they were in the vanguard for the idea in Britain. Nevertheless, Packard chose to announce to the US market in 1909 that it now offered the European trend: engine before the driver. Packard supported the European arguments and added driver safety and comfort. Packard's lead was soon imitated by White, Peerless, Pierce-Arrow and the bulk of the market within less than five years. During that time engineers, journalists, operators and drivers pronounced emphatically one way or another. All had undeniable evidence that cab-over or driver behind the engine was better or worse, and the argument raged on both sides of the Atlantic.

The importance of Packard's empire must be reflected in a survey of 1911 which showed that the company had 7% of the truck market, and to try to boost this figure yet further the company announced its intentions in November that year of offering discounts to buyers on a sliding discount basis. Those who ordered more got bigger discounts. The company also expanded its scope with a $1\frac{1}{2}$-ton range. A few months later, on July 8th, 1912, a lone Packard truck departed from New York and on August 24th arrived in San Francisco, gaining the honour of being the first truck to cross the United States continent from east to west.

The company finally got around to changing to left-hand steering and worm drive with the 1915 range, coinciding with a

general tendency throughout the industry. Whereas in 1913 70% of US trucks still had right-hand steering, the percentage had dropped to 43% in 1915. Likewise, chains, which had a 79% grip of the market in 1913, had dropped to 50%. This new range involved the company in £250,000 re-tooling costs for what was considered as Packard's ultimate achievement in the truck market. In addition, this range boasted the introduction of the L-head engine design, rated in Packard's case at 32.4 hp. Packard truck sales well exceeded those of private cars during 1918 – due, of course, to the wartime conditions. That aside, little did Packard know it, nor perhaps many other manufacturers, but the day of the truck had arrived. When war was over, there would be no return to competition between the horse and the truck. The truck had proved its worth and the horse was dead, at least in the States. US truck manufacturers were on the threshold of a boom that, after an initial lull, would never stop escalating. New highways were under construction, and together with pneumatic tyres for 3-ton loads, had increased the speed of the truck so that not only did it render the horse obsolete, but also the great railroad networks. Packard, unfortunately, were never to share in this wealth. The company's share of the truck market had fallen to only 2% by 1920 and Alvan Macauley, who took over the presidency at Packard in April 1917, decided in 1922 to quit the truck market in order to concentrate on high-class automobiles – the last Packard truck rolling off the line in 1923.

PIERCE-ARROW

1911 was perhaps a landmark in the history of the truck for it was the year in which there were signs of a significant gain over public prejudice. In Boston, Mass., plans were put forward to exclude the horse entirely from certain streets. At last it was realised that horses were not only responsible for congestion but were a hazard to public health. Foul streets, blow-flies and dirt in shops were all directly attributable to the horse. In Maine, proposals went even further: entire streets should be devoted solely to the motor truck or trolleycar. Sixty years later this proposal is being made again in almost every city in the world yet not even in Maine has it been adopted. Yet it appeared that the insurance companies were still dragging behind public thinking – they insisted on an added premium of 50% if gasoline trucks entered steamship or railroad wharves.

It was in 1911, too, that the famous luxury automobile company, Pierce-Arrow, whose long history included birdcage and bicycle manufacture, decided to enter the truck market. This entry heralded a new trend for the American truck. Pierce-Arrow brought to the market another European trait, the overslung worm rear axle in a 5-tonner. Until now live axles had been confined to the lighter range of commercials. Overhead worm allowed the whole reduction to be done in one stage, instead of part in the right angle drive and part in the chain, and of course, it was quieter and more substantial.

And so began another round of debates. Chains were lighter, cheaper, gave better ground clearance and reduced the deadweight, it was reasoned. Arguments aside, other manufacturers were quick to copy Pierce-Arrow, though many Americans were convinced that the worm added to deadweight and this increased the popularity of the Torbensen system in the States.

The Pierce-Arrow truck division was set up under the direction of two brilliant engineers, H K Thomas and John Younger. A prototype cab-over-engine model did a gruelling 10-day test over most New York and Pennsylvania state roads before production began. This prototype showed up many weaknesses in design,

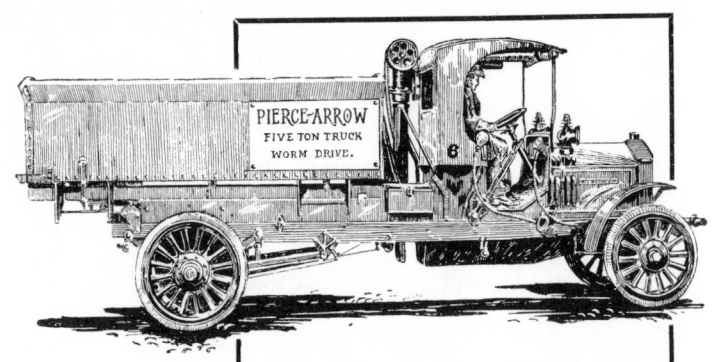

QUALITY

The Pierce-Arrow chassis embodies the best and most modern principles of commercial vehicle engineering, carried out in the thorough and characteristic manner which has made Pierce-Arrow productions known and respected in all parts of the world. It is indisputably the finest example yet placed on the market, and although the initial cost is a trifle high, its unfailing reliability—low running costs—and hard wearing qualities make it cheapest in the end.

PIERCE-ARROW

The Acme of Engineering Perfection.

2 TON, £745.   5 TON, £1,085.

Consult us if you want large fleets for
IMMEDIATE DELIVERY.

Gaston, Williams & Wigmore, Ltd.

Alexandra House, Kingsway, London, W.C.

Telephone—Regent 550 (three lines).

Pierce-Arrow trucks were offered to the British market during the Great War.
Commercial Motor – March 1916

particularly having the cab over the engine, which made Pierce opt for the new vogue in bonneted design.

The first sale was to the International Brewing Corporation. This truck attracted immediate renown by travelling, fully loaded, from New York to Boston (231 miles) in 20 hours. In 1918 the same truck was still working for International Brewing, having covered 130,000-odd miles to its credit. Pierce thought it a good publicity stunt if it could do the same New York to Boston journey once again. It did. This time in 18 hrs 7 mins. To top this achievement the driver lost his way, adding some minutes to the journey, and nine miles had been added to the route by the introduction of a detour!

Within a couple of years of this first truck having left the factory, Pierce had made themselves a name in the trucking industry equal to that in the automobile world.

After war broke out in Europe, Pierce truck sales increased still further by the demand from British hauliers unable to buy home-built trucks. In Britain at that time they were expensive (£1,805 for the 5-ton model), but even so they sold well in advance of supplies. The Cerebos Salt truck illustrated (**69**) is one of those from the 1915 contingent.

They were also liked by the French and British armies and when the United States entered the war record numbers were built – over 7,000 just for the year 1918.

The anti-climax was swift. Things had changed with the war. Many of Pierce's affluent customers had gone forever – the extravagant Pierce 66 automobile that gobbled up a gallon of petrol every four miles was 'out' with the new generation, as was the glitter that went hand in glove with Pierce. What's more, the balance sheets were also fading and a new post-war management had none of the pre-war grace. They were bankers – there for the short-term profit. They were last of all car or engineering men. Even the old personnel fell, one by one, by the wayside.

One 'old school' engineer, Francis Davis, was now to be found as Chief Engineer of the truck plant. Davis had served in that section since its inception and, in fact, drive-tested the prototype. Writer Maurice Hendry credits him with having invented power steering in later years, although Davis said he first realised the need whilst driving the prototype.

Sales continued to slip for a while at Pierce, particularly on the truck side, which never regained its former eminence, despite many 'new' variations of the original design. A 2, $2\frac{1}{2}$, 3, $3\frac{1}{2}$, 4, 5

and 6½-ton range made up the catalogue – whilst 4-speed replaced the old 3-speed gearboxes. The 38 hp T-head engine remained basic until 1924 when Pierce announced a 6-cylinder dual valve engine in a drop-frame bus chassis that was also sold as a fire truck and intercity freight van.

Two years later the cheap Series 80 car units were used in the make-up of a new 'Fleet Arrow' line of trucks powered by a 6-cylinder L-head engine. Sales of the 'Fleet Arrow' and dual valve models were low. None of the post-war offerings gave Pierce-Arrow back their original truck world status and by 1927 the Pierce name as builders of trucks had really started to become just another legend.

SENTINEL – ALLEY & MacLELLAN

Basically steam lorries, or wagons as they were usually referred to, were divided up into two main types: the horizontal boiler (overtype) design and the vertical boiler (undertype). There was also, of course, the cross-boiler, of which Yorkshire were the principal exponents. If it had ended there, it would have been simple. Many inventors and engineers, as well as those with more money than sense, tried their hand at finding ways. The majority, if they got beyond the drawing board, never succeeded in producing more than a handful of vehicles. The main types, loco and undertype, were even divided into segments. Leyland and Fowler, for example, fitted fire tube boilers whilst Sentinel and Garrett decided on water-tube boilers. To ask which of the many types of wagon was best is almost asking for the impossible. To be able to answer the question one would have to have had a large fleet with the various types running side by side, or to have driven all the various types. As most firms stayed with the same make, or the drivers kept to the same wagon, there were few who could truthfully give the answer then and even fewer today.

One thing is sure, Sentinel far outsold any other wagon and remained in business, selling steam long after everybody else. Their success seems to have been, firstly ease of maintenance. The boiler was very accessible and this feature alone always went down well with the drivers or fitters.

Secondly, Sentinel had the advantage over all other manufacturers in that they had a good number of service depots up and down the country. Thirdly, Sentinel were one of the few undertypes that could maintain a good head of steam, due to their first rate superheater – unlike Garrett, for example, whose superheater was good but only while it lasted, a primitive sort of 'built-in obsolescence'. Lastly, the Sentinel was cheaper than any of its rivals.

The Sentinel was the product of a well-established marine engineering firm by the name of Alley & MacLellan of Glasgow. Their experiments with steam wagons commenced in 1904 and their first wagon, an undertype, was shown at the 1906 Brewers'

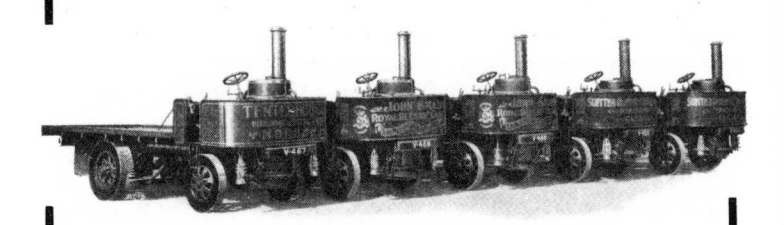
An early advertisement for Sentinel undertype steam wagons.

Exhibition. Sentinel remained faithful to their undertype principle right to the end in 1950, with a brief dabble at the overtype in 1911.

To quote from Maurice Kelly's book *The Overtype Steam Wagon*: 'It was an undeniable fact in the pre-First World War period that the overtype was a far better proposition thermally than the average undertype, but also, that the Sentinel wagon was a great deal better than average; so in order to attempt to prove that their standard vehicle was the most superior wagon on the road, bar none, the company produced the most carefully constructed and well-designed overtype, virtually regardless of cost, and then proceeded to compare it with their normal product. They set out to show through their advertising that as their overtype was at least as good as everyone else's, and as their undertype was better than their own overtype, it must follow that the undertype was better than the overtype! One of these advertisements of 1917 reads "The Sentinel Works once built overtype wagons of the ordinary traction-engine pattern, but this type was, after exhaustive trials, definitely discarded five years ago in favour of the improved original undertype – built like a motorcar; driven like a motorcar; running like a motorcar".'

Alley & MacLellan had far outgrown their Glasgow premises by the outbreak of war and as most of their sales were south of the border, the decision was taken to move south and build a large enough factory. With the move in 1915 came the chance to segregate the business and set up a new company – Sentinel Waggon Works Ltd. The most unlikely town one could ever imagine as a manufacturing centre for one of the world's largest and longest-lived producers of steam wagons is mediaeval Shrewsbury, county town of Shropshire, which is still very sleepy and old-world.

When Alley & MacLellan decided to buy a 65-acre site almost in the heart of Shrewsbury, there was a riot in the council boardroom and residents objected strongly. Only the war and a sense of national duty allowed the building of the factory to go through.

At Shrewsbury the business continued to expand even more. There was no sign of a let-up in the popularity of the steam wagon, even though other countries had abandoned steam in the first decade of the century. After the war, demands for home fuel became stronger and it became evident that the undertype was a more practicable proposition. The overtype did, after all, take up a lot of valuable space, adding to dead costs. Competitive manu-

facturers also began to see the light of day and tried their hand at producing undertypes. None had much commercial success. Atkinson were probably the only manufacturer to build and sell in any quantity worth considering, and that was a negligible figure compared with Sentinel. Sentinel's rivals had left it too late to switch horses and by the twenties, most customers interested in steam wagons knew they could get their best deal, based on experience, from Sentinel.

THORNYCROFT

The law in Britain, compelling a man to precede a road vehicle with a red flag, had been repealed in 1878, but the rest of the restrictions making up the Act, including a 4 mph maximum speed, were to continue until 1896. No sooner had the Act been completely repealed than countless numbers of small machine shops, marine engineers and bicycle businesses took positive steps to develop and sell viable road machines. Not that anyone beat a path to the manufacturers' doors – it was the other way round. Manufacturers had to cut through years of prejudice to prove their products were reliable and could do the job better than the horse.

One of the first to announce their intentions of building self-propelled road vehicles was the Chiswick engineering firm, J I Thornycroft. John I Thornycroft actually claimed to have designed a steam carriage in the early 1860s. Indeed it was his cherished desire to build this coach and obvious foresight in anticipating that the law would be changed that prompted Thornycroft to build a van propelled by a water-tube boiler and launch engine. When the Act was fully repealed this was the only British self-propelled industrial vehicle able to take freely to the road. There were not many home-built passenger cars either. Most that turned up for the 1896 Crystal Palace Motor Show and the Emancipation Run were of foreign construction. Thornycroft got a head start over everyone else in the steam wagon field, including the Lancashire Steam Motor Company. Within a couple of years Thornycroft orders and achievements warranted the purchase of some land at Basingstoke in Hampshire. They were in the fore-front supplying wagons to municipalities as early as 1897, and to many leading stores and businesses, and they did remarkably well at every trial they entered, gold medals being won at Crystal Palace in 1896, Richmond and Dover in 1899, Glasgow in 1904 and at Liverpool in 1899 and 1901. The company secured an order from the War Office for a handful of wagons to be shipped to South Africa where the Boer Rising was being fought. Kitchener paid the highest tribute possible, 'The motor lorries sent to Africa did well; Thornycrofts are best'.

Thornycroft sent an engineer to South Africa to study the performance of the wagons. The experience and observations obtained were then put into the designing of a special model that could be used in under-developed countries, where roads were non-existent and fuel indifferent – unlike the good Welsh coal found at home. The company was not slow to realise the potential within the great British Empire and exports accounted for a very large proportion of their sales.

When the new 5-ton export model was offered in 1902 what could have been a more simple yet patriotic name than the 'Colonial' model? To the lay observer the most striking difference was in the extra ground clearance and the extra transverse spring at the front. The 3-point spring mounting and tilting axle were the main features designed to absorb the shocks of unmade roads or elephant tracks. Exports of the Colonial model were made to places as widespread as New Zealand, Africa, the United States and Canada, India, Burma, Malay and Mauritius.

The Thornycroft standard 4-ton wagon continued to be the most popular on the home market and by 1903 some 100 wagons a year were leaving the factory – a lot in those days. A new 5-ton model was added to the catalogue in 1904. The most notable feature was a pistol-shaped locomotive boiler in place of Thornycroft's usual water-tubed vertical boiler. The engine was retained in a dust-proof, oil-tight casing similar to that used on the Colonial model. The final drive, as on most Thornycrofts, was via an all-gear-driven transmission. Chains were found to be unsatisfactory for heavy wagons by Thornycroft (along with certain other British wagon builders) very early in the company's history.

Despite having been at the forefront of the wagon trade, Thornycroft in 1907 elected to drop the steam side of their business in favour of the petrol engine. Licence to continue the manufacture of Thornycroft steam wagons was granted to Duncan Stewart (a firm who also built their own wagons) of Glasgow. The directors must have had a good deal of courage and foresight to make such a clear-cut decision. They had only entered the internal combustion market in 1902 and although they were doing reasonably well, no one could say their sales outshone those of any other manufacturer or justified abandoning steam. Undoubtedly, the directors having been utterly convinced that the future lay with motor vehicles, decided to concentrate all their efforts on the motor vehicle and be done with steam for ever.

The highlight of the petrol-engined commercial vehicle was the

3-4 ton subsidy chassis developed in 1912, widely known as the J-type. A distinctive feature was the inversely dished steel wheels which offset the steering knuckles so that the king pins were aligned with the wheel planes – also a feature of the new 1913 twin-shaft Austin. Cast metal wheels were mostly used in Britain at that time – a scarcity of wood being given as one reason, although this is difficult to accept. The cast spoked wheel was, at this time, becoming popular both sides of the Atlantic. Wooden wheels on large vehicles got out of round and pressed steel wheels started to go out of fashion, for they lacked lateral strength and buckled when driven against the kerb. Even so, many of the J-types had the pressed steel dished wheel and these were a distinguishable feature of those used by the War Department.

At the War's end, Thornycroft decided to introduce no new designs, perhaps a wise move in view of the many surplus trucks available. There were, of course, improvements to the regular production, and they won the 1921 Dewar Trophy with a 2-ton model. But taking the twenties as a whole, Thornycroft designs became staid and they lost their lead. They did, however, grow richer. Sales from Commonwealth and other overseas countries probably far exceeded those of any other British make.

One field in which Thornycroft attempted to make progress was the development of the rigid 6-wheeled chassis. The rigid 6-wheeler had originated in the States and much groundwork was done by Goodyear Tyres. Basically it was thought that the rigid 6-wheeler had the advantage in spreading the load, reducing the tare weights on each axle, increasing the length to accommodate extra load space, smoother riding and reduced tyre wear. In fact, the latter was one area where the 6-wheeler did not score. Scuffing and wheel spin caused excess tyre wear, added to which it was common for the front wheel of the rear bogie to scrape horse-shoe nails from the road at high speed, which punctured the rearmost tyre. It seems that only the tyre companies really made any profit from the 6-wheeler. Moreland were to the fore in the States, and the Thornycroft A3 model was perhaps the most advanced on the British market in 1926.

TILLING-STEVENS

The oldest London bus operator until nationalisation in 1933 was Thomas Tilling Ltd. Started in 1847 by a young and energetic general dealer, Thomas Tilling, in the village of Peckham (now part of South-East London), this business did well enough during the Great Exhibition of 1851 to establish Tilling as a flourishing young horse bus operator. Throughout the next fifty years the Thomas Tilling business grew to become not only respected horse bus proprietors but the largest breeders and hirers of horses in Great Britain. Tilling's famous 'Greys' were used for Royal and State occasions, for funerals, for mail and general haulage. At the turn of the century, Tilling's name was an established household word. Thoroughly respectable, they smacked of the wealth synonymous with the best of the British Empire. The business was still a family affair and controlled by grandson Richard Tilling.

Soon after the turn of the century Tillings' trunk route from the West End through South London to Peckham was overshadowed by the new electric trams. As if competition from the new rates-subsidised electric monsters was not enough, next came the new motor buses to further add to the trouble. Tillings were one of the first London bus concerns to buy motorbuses, but the motorbuses gave more than their fair share of trouble. Healthy balance sheets disappeared almost overnight. Horse drivers had no idea how to handle motors, mechanics were virtually non-existent and stable lads, vets, ostlers and all the numbers of men whose life was entirely devoted to the horse, found themselves lost and without jobs in a new world.

Tillings meant to keep as many of their old staff as possible. They were determined to try and find an easier vehicle for their men to drive. Gear changing had been the prime difficulty, causing many lesser men, unable to adapt themselves to the new art, to fall by the wayside and become mere beerhouse flops. If gear changing could be made easier, many good men could be kept in employment – and anyway qualified motor drivers were hard to come by.

Various firms had ideas on the subject. Some opted for the

primitive pre-selective gearboxes, others for friction drive, or you could settle for steam or battery power. In the United States some pioneers propounded the idea of having the petrol engine provide the power and an electric motor provide the drive. Petrol or gas-electrics, as they were known in the States, had their advantages, being basically smooth on take-off and easy to drive. Another factor that became evident was the saving of wear and tear on the transmission. Early commercial vehicles (buses in particular) suffered severely from transmission failure. Teeth or pinions quickly wore down under stress and, indeed, some vehicles spent one day in seven having parts replaced.

There were a number of American chassis imported into England, the first seeming to have been in 1903, promoting the petrol-electric principle. The Daimler Company at Coventry became interested in the idea around 1906–7; Wolseley and BTH got their heads together, but all to no avail. Then in 1906 Tillings having been introduced to a Mr W A Stevens at the Olympia Commercial Vehicle Exhibition, they asked him to cooperate with their chief engineer, Percy Frost-Smith. Stevens's electrical firm in Maidstone, Kent, had already converted his motorcar to petrol-electric a year earlier. The first result of the collaboration was in 1908 when a modified Hallford bus chassis converted to electric drive commenced bus service for Tillings. This success led to a Milnes-Daimler chassis being adapted to the same principle, although battery driven. W A Stevens continued with their conversions, undertaking four Dennis chassis – two of which went to India and two to Holland. After two years of exhaustive tests, Thomas Tilling decided to go wholeheartedly for the idea. Agreements were made with Messrs W A Stevens to supply chassis to Thomas Tilling, who in turn would build the bus bodies and operate them.

The first of the new chassis appeared in June 1911 – it was a Tilling-Stevens Model Type TTA1. This code surely needs no explanation! Tillings replaced the remainder of their horse service and then all the various standard-drive buses with the new TTA1s within a few months. The TTA1s gave way to improved designs and the Tilling-Stevens petrol-electrics became the only vehicles operated by Thomas Tilling in 1930.

As soon as W A Stevens had supplied enough buses to Thomas Tilling to replace all the remaining horses and other motor bus types, the chassis became more readily available to other bus and haulage users. At the Maidstone factory eventually everything

Paying Points of the Petrol Electric.

Simplicity is the keynote of the control of the Petrol-Electric. All speeds are achieved and controlled by the resistance lever on the steering column—the Driver's attention can therefore be entirely concentrated on steering, a very vital operation, particularly in congested traffic districts.

The petrol engine is, mechanically, absolutely isolated from the differential gear and back axle. No road shocks can possibly be transmitted direct to the engine—consequent low maintenance is ensured and added life to the entire vehicle.

Tilling-Stevens Petrol-Electric is a mobile self-contained electric generating plant. When the vehicle comes to rest, the driving gear can be switched into operation as a power plant. The auxiliary uses available are applied with success to Mobile Arc Welding Equipment, Mobile Cinematograph Outfit, Tilling-Stevens Patent Fire Engine, and Mobile Petrol-Electric Cranes.

Clutch and gear box are entirely eliminated, affording immunity from damage to chassis by faulty gear changing and abrupt clutch usage. This principle also minimises driving operations and ensures steady running under all conditions.

The petrol electric explained.

ASE OF CONTROL.

NO MECHANICAL CONNECTION BETWEEN
ENGINE AND BACK AXLE.

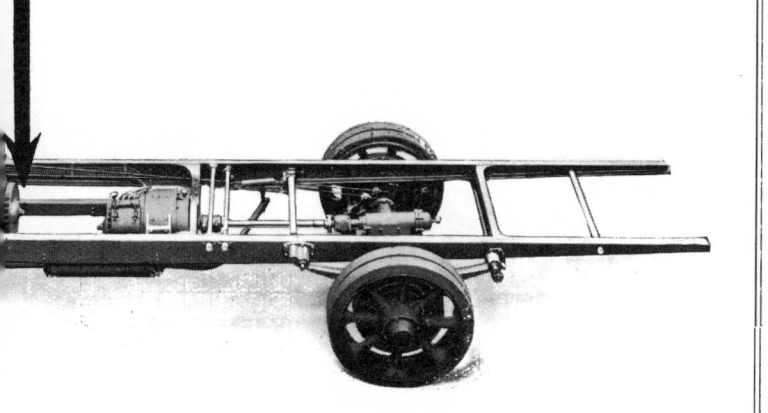

ELECTRICAL POWER AVAILABLE FOR
AUXILIARY USES.

GEARS, NOR CLUTCH.

mechanical was made within the works, without relying on any outside suppliers – this included the engine. The system had its disadvantages, of course. It was a heavy chassis with all its electrical gear and expensive compared with other vehicles. W A Stevens no doubt realised this problem, for in 1914 they offered in addition the TTB1 and TTB2 – 1 and 2 ton gear-driven vehicles. Thereafter, standard gearbox transmission vehicles were offered continuously until 1952, when the company's control was assumed by Tilling's close affinity with the production side was reflected in August 1915 when they purchased stock in a newly formed public company, named Tilling-Stevens Ltd, which absorbed the assets of W A Stevens Ltd. There had been experiments with petrol-electric trams in 1913 and there were efforts to market petrol-electric trolleybuses in the mid-twenties, but it was for the sale of motor-buses that the company was most widely known.

Whilst Tilling-Stevens were the major producers of petrol-electrics in Britain and had no rivals worth mentioning, in the States several firms marketed the system. Generally speaking in America, the chassis were sold for passenger work and, occasionally, for fire trucks. As more refined transmission systems developed in the twenties, the petrol-electric lost favour. Even so, Mr W A Stevens, who had departed from Tilling-Stevens in 1917, continued to show faith in the idea. He reasoned that with the advent of the less flexible oil engine, the electric transmission will prove ideal. 'It will enable the engine to be run at constant speed and, at the same time, allow the vehicle to be run at any speed between zero and maximum. There can be no limit to the number of road wheels that can be driven, as an electric motor can be provided for each axle,' stated Stevens. At an appeal put to the House of Lords, they unanimously decided that the petrol-electric vehicle was confirmed to be 'electrically propelled' within the meaning of the 1926 Finance Act. This authorised the taxation of goods-carrying petrol-electrics at a rate approximately half that of gear-driven vehicles of the same load capacity. Not even a tax saving could convince enough buyers, so Tilling-Stevens were faced with no alternative but to start to discontinue the electric transmission from regular production by 1929. However, orders still trickled in whilst the War Department were the last to receive petrol-electrics between 1936 and 1942.

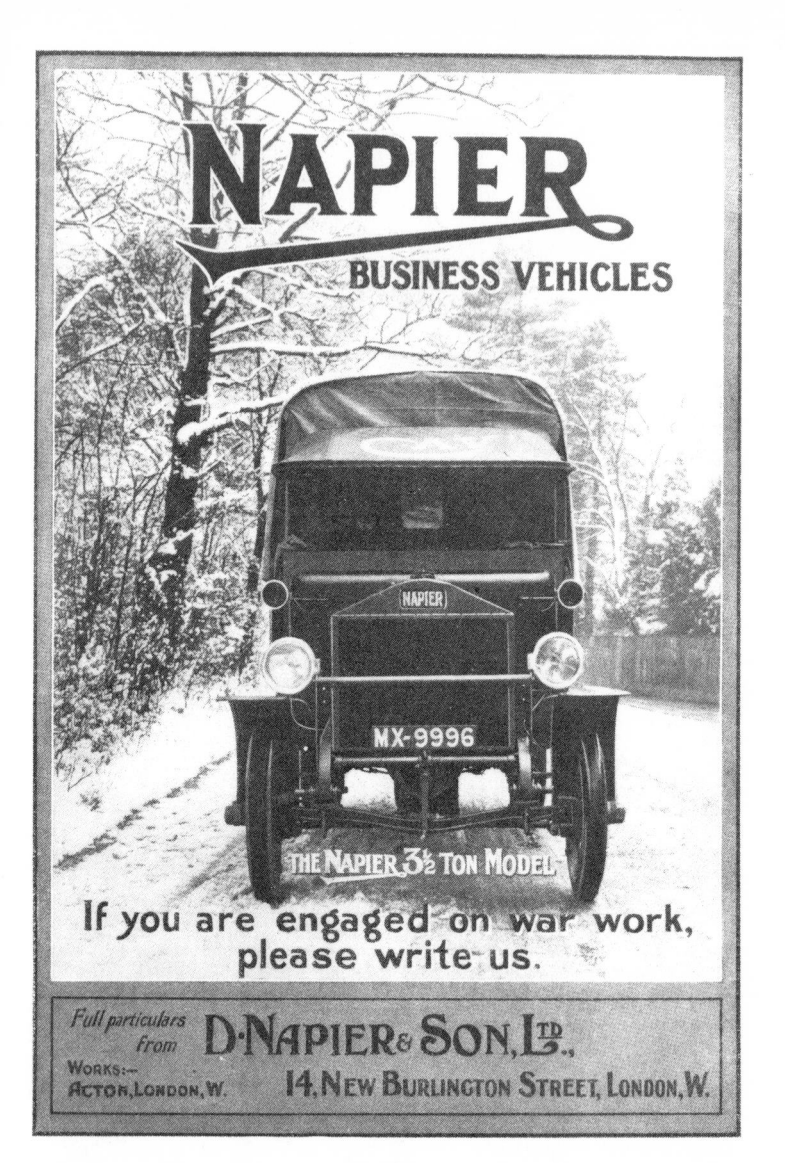

Some of the nicest advertising of the Great War period came from Napiers – at a time when Napier were pushing their truck sales above all their other products.

Commercial Motor – March 1916

WHERE TO SEE OLD COMMERCIALS

The collecting of old trucks and buses is, at the moment, a thriving hobby only in Britain, the major institution being the Historic Commercial Vehicle Club, founded in 1958. The most important role of this Club is the organisation of the London to Brighton Run, held annually on the first Sunday in May – exactly six months after (or before) the Veteran Car Run that commemorates the final repealing of the Red Flag Act in 1896.

On this first Sunday in May about 180 aged trucks, fire engines, buses, ambulances, vans, etc. line up at Battersea Park from around 6.30 am. The first departure at 8 am is usually one of the slower iron-tyred steam wagons and by 9.30 am the newer buses of the thirties are on their way. At Brighton the vehicles start to arrive mid-morning and are displayed for public inspection until late afternoon. Ever since the first Run in 1962 there has been brilliant sunshine for the event and each year the sightseeing traffic that ventures on the Brighton road to see the Run has increased so much that the actual entrants now have difficulty reaching Brighton by lunchtime!

The HCVC's other important function is to offer members insurance at very keen rates – otherwise members are left to form little cliques among themselves. The Club is very poor at organising regular meetings, lectures, library research and educational visits.

Throughout the summer there are numerous traction engine rallies, many of which welcome commercial vehicles. The Midland Festival of Steam in July and the Grand Transport Extravaganza at the Crich Tramway Museum over the August Bank Holiday are two events where commercials can be found in abundance.

The Northern equivalent to the London to Brighton Run is the Trans-Pennine Run from Manchester to Harrogate, usually held on the second Sunday in August.

The one museum that had a fair smattering of trucks was the Museum of British Transport at Clapham. There were a number of former railway company owned trucks, but these were either put into store or passed over to members of the Historic Com-

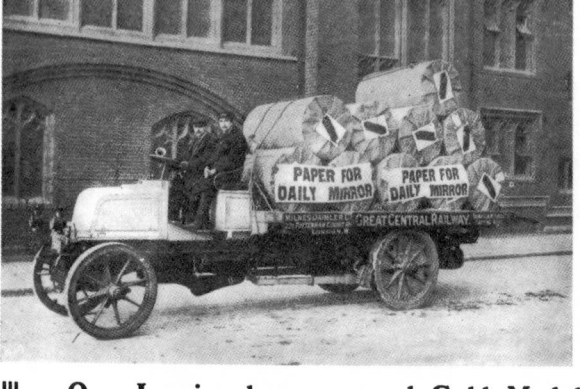
The German Daimler as was marketed in England by G F Milnes.

Commercial Motor – February 1906

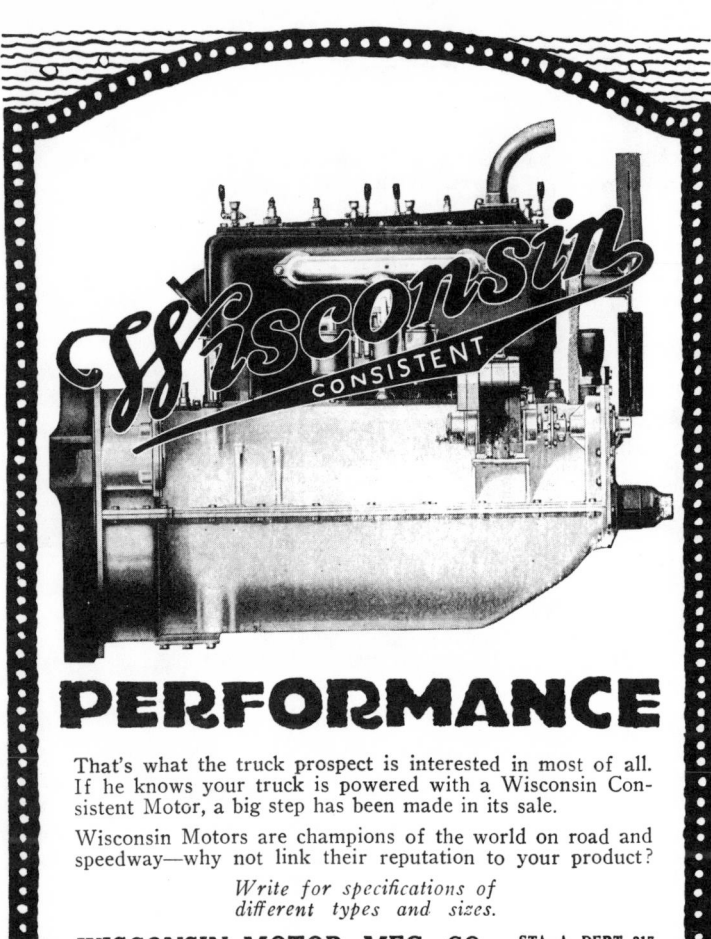
Wisconsin were fourth in the charts among the loose-engine manufacturers.
Motor – January 1918

mercial Vehicle Club around 1966, leaving the museum bereft of trucks. Other museums in Britain seem very slow to appreciate the truck's appeal. The Science Museum offers nothing, whilst the Montagu Motor Museum has an exceptionally dull handful, tucked to one side and treated rather like fairground curiosities.

Efforts to get a commercial vehicle club going in the United States have proved abortive so far. The Antique Automobile Club of America hold trucks seminars at their Annual General Meetings, which usually last a long weekend. Most of those attending the truck seminars are frustrated at being a small band within a big club that really has not much interest in the truck. Then, again, many of the trucks preserved in the States which appear at rallies are gaudily painted 'popcorn' or 'pie' vans – none ever seem to be taken seriously enough by their owners to represent an authentic period truck.

One of the more serious collectors of trucks in the United States is Henry Austin Clark, Jr of Southampton, Long Island. Austin Clark has a fair sized museum, with a number of trucks and buses represented. Sad though it may be to read, many of these are in a bad state of repair and take second place to the automobiles.

One US collector who takes the art more seriously is Phil Bomgarten at Jackson, Michigan. Mr Bomgarten has early examples of Whites, Autocars, Kelly Springfields, Brockways, Diamond Ts and Pierce-Arrows and usually restores them to an authentic standard. His collection is not open to the public, but invariably callers giving some advance notice are accorded a warm welcome.

In Australia plenty of trucks are still to be found in the outback, and many are being snapped up at bargain prices by collectors. This collecting of commercials is at the stage Britain was about 1958. The national club, the Historic Commercial Vehicle Club of Australia, has a staunch band of members but distance seems the greatest obstacle when organising meetings and rallies.

Throughout Europe one finds it hard to locate any enthusiasts or collectors of trucks and these lie rotting in places like French farmyards and are offered to anyone interested at usually ridiculously cheap prices.

Tillotson

CARBURETOR

ENGINEERS and manufacturers of motor cars and motor trucks who are familiar with the Tillotson design of carburetor know that for downright dependability and all-around efficiency it cannot be excelled.

Over 300,000 are in use today!

Tillotsons are giving carburetor satisfaction to owners of cars of varying power, size and weight. Each model is specially designed and built for the particular type of car it is to serve.

Let us figure on your requirements for the coming year.

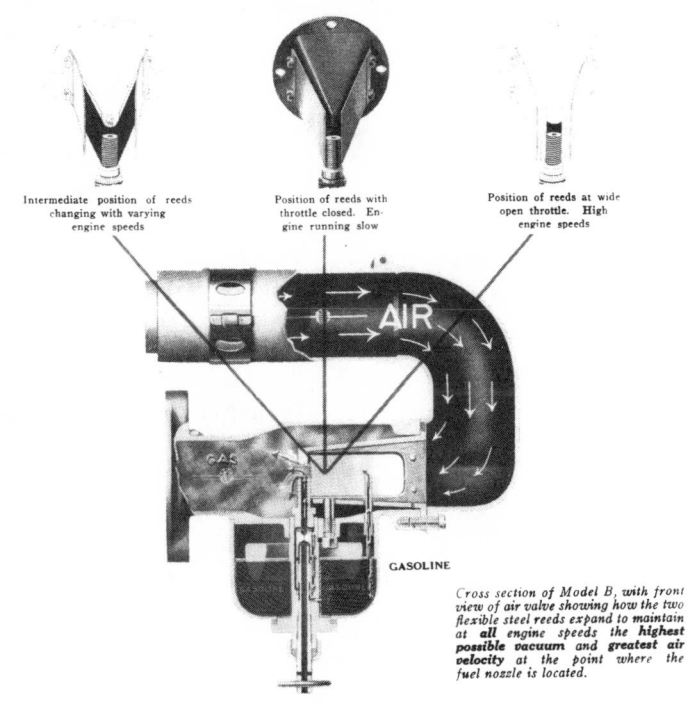

Intermediate position of reeds changing with varying engine speeds

Position of reeds with throttle closed. Engine running slow

Position of reeds at wide open throttle. High engine speeds

AIR

GAS

GASOLINE

*Cross section of Model B, with front view of air valve showing how the two flexible steel reeds expand to maintain at **all** engine speeds the **highest possible vacuum** and **greatest air velocity** at the point where the fuel nozzle is located.*

The Tillotson Manufacturing Company
Toledo, Ohio

Sixty years ago Commer were aware of the future potential of the truck.
Motor Trader – April 1908

GLOVER BROS., Ltd.,
28, CLEVELAND STREET,
LONDON. W.

MOTOR VAN & OMNIBUS BUILDERS.

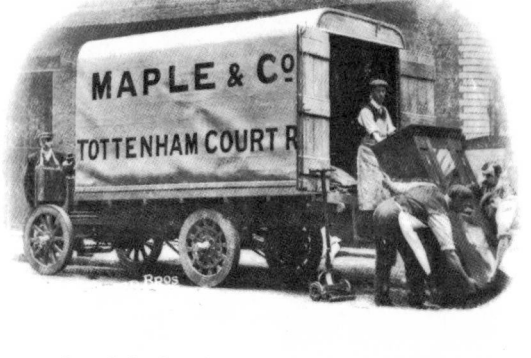

I, 2 & 3 Ton Loads.

~

**VEHICLES
KEPT IN
REPAIR BY
CONTRACT.**

~

Trial Runs
can be
arranged by
appointment.

Most popular of the London based body builders were Glover Brothers, still in business today as Glover, Webb and Liversidge. They even tried their hand at making their own chassis.

Commercial Motor – September 1905